English for the Media

Latha Nair

Priya K Nair
Vidhu Mary John
Shelton Pinheiro

FOUNDATION
BOOKS

FOUNDATION BOOKS

Foundation Books is an imprint of Cambridge University Press India Pvt. Ltd.

314 to 321, 3rd Floor, Plot No. 3, Splendor Forum, Jasola District Centre, New Delhi – 110025, India

www.cambridgeindia.org

First published 2014
Reprint 2016, 2018, 2019, 2020, 2021

Printed in India by Magic International Pvt. Ltd., Greater Noida

ISBN 978-93-82993-49-0 Paperback

Contents

Preface

English for Media provides a comprehensive introduction to the use of English in the world of media. The invasion of the new media (television and internet) has introduced perceptible changes in the language, style, design and content writing. This book is designed for giving the learners an insight into how English is used in Print, Visual & Digital Media, Radio and Advertising. The themed sections start with the basics; they explain why we need to look at language use critically, so as to understand the syntactic processes involved in making writing for media a highly specialized subject. Writing for media involves special skills and sensitization as far as language use is concerned. The main focus of this book is on sensitizing the learners about the need for using more polished and refined language as feature writers in various key topics like, say, culture, cinema, art, literature, fashion, cuisine, defence, rural affairs etc. The chapters are conceived in a different way with interactive work sections and in-depth exercises to enable them to research facts and collate them, as a part of their writing. The glossary provides an insight into all the important media and advertising terms. Care has been taken to make the language learner friendly and accessible for all types of learners.

Anyone who engages in this kind of academic practice knows about people who contribute and create a conducive atmosphere, making you feel that their support is invaluable. In this respect I would like to mention the names of Dr. P. J. Jacob, Chairman of the Board of Studies of Kerala University, who trusted me with the task and gave me an opening; Roshan Thomas (Cambridge University Press) whose firm and patient encouragement made this book evolve and Pradeep, my friend at *The Hindu*, whose experience provided a lot of incisive comments that were invaluable sources of insight and confirmation for writing the Introduction.

It remains to thank the authors who were more than patient and my colleagues Dr. Priya K Nair, Ms. Vidhu Mary John for their galvanizing energy and ideas. It is their commitment and unbounded optimism that made this book look at the wider social affordances of language use in contemporary media. I was indeed blessed to 'drag' the creative, insightful contributor Shelton Pinhero who heads the Stark Communications as the National Creative Director to contribute for the section on Advertising. I would like to specially thank Shelton for providing us with beautiful photographs that he used for the launch of *Mazhavil Manorama*.

Introduction

Newspapers are a part of our lives. The world and the word get connected through this powerful medium. The invasion of the new media (television and internet) has introduced perceptible changes in the language, style and design of newspapers. The floodgates have opened and there is news everywhere. You don't have to depend upon the newspaper anymore to connect with the world. The news that comes to you in the morning has no freshness. So, the newspapers had to evolve a new methodology to catch up and beat the new media.

What now captures the pertinent eye is the fact that the news is no longer simply reported. They are no longer essays that are stuffed with facts, names, dates and stereotypical content. It has become more analytical, more featurish. The demand is to get the details of a happening or an event that has already been reported.

This has demanded an overall change. What Clarence Barron, former editor of *Wall Street Journal* once said is true today: 'The soul of all writing', he said, 'its use and beauty is the animation of the writer to serve the reader. Never write from the standpoint of yourself but always from the reader. Economise his time and crowd the most important facts and determining factors into the smallest possible compass that will carry truth to the brain, remembering that the frame is always part of the picture.'

Let's look at some sensational news headlines: Sreesanth puts IPL in a spot, fans in a fix, A game of bet and Ball, red faced congress axes Aswani Kumar, Bansal ....

Feature writing has now evolved as a highly specialized subject. What was once considered a non-news article on some subject has now moved into the realm of hard news. Newspapers have specialized feature writers in various key topics like culture, cinema, art, literature, fashion, cusine defence and rural affairs. The language in features tends to become more polished and refined. This is because the writer gets more time at his/her disposal to research on facts and collate them. Of course, there are times when the writer needs to file the story within a short deadline. In these cases perhaps his/her training helps. Here you feel that Aristotle's theory comes into force in writing styles. Unconsciously or deliberately, there is a perfect beginning, middle and an end to his/her story. This feature style is being widely used in reporting today.

Op-ed and editorial styles have not changed much. These are two 'serious' pages but the aforementioned demands have had its impact here too. The writing has become crisp unlike the long winding essays we were used to reading. There are more photographs, cartoons or caricature sometimes on these pages. Instead of the holy, in-house edit writer we now have experts in various fields commenting on these pages. And, even in these cases the wordage is very specifically determined. The writing styles, in terms of language, is much more sacrosanct and correct and the words or turn of phrases used very often more complex than a new report.

Interviews are a part of feature writing, but you may seriously think at times whether they are going out of 'fashion'. This is in vogue when it comes to talking to very important personalities, like heads of state or corporates, who demand the questions in advance. Very often the person writes down the answers. It is also used in e-mail or telephonic interviews. Another aspect in this field is using a statement or a heading followed by the first person answers. For example, in an interview with Amitabh Bachchan you just put 'Best Film' and the answers follow. The Proust Interview, introduced by *The Hindu MetroPlus* is a refreshing change in this interview sector.

The challenge that the writer faces today is to adapt to changing styles. Someone honed to the regular reporting style and language may find it a bit difficult to switch over to the more featurish one. There is no room for just stating facts as it happens. The need is to go deeper into a story, get fresh insights and new angles; and all this must be presented in a refreshingly readable language style. If the reader fails to go beyond the first two paragraphs of the story your effort has failed. And if readers keep telling you that they enjoyed what you have written, your work is well done. The challenge is to find something new in something already reported or in something that has happened and to make your reader sit down and read your copy.

Writing headlines is an art. It comes with practice. In fact, this is the job of the people on the desk, the editors. A story can be elevated or marred by the use of a headline. Remember that there are many who read only the headlines in the newspaper and this must lead him or her to the rest of the story. Usually the active verbs are left out in headlines; the articles are also usually left out. Only well-known abbreviations should be used. The punctuation marks, especially the comma has effective use. Instead of punning on words, which is an obsolete style, especially when resorted to frequently, a headline should capture the essence of the story. This means that the editor or the people on the desk need to go through the copy very carefully, capture the soul and then think of a headline.

English is a foreign language in India. Under the circumstances our newspapers handle the language as well and even better than the true blood English products. Yes, there has been a significant decline in the use of the language. The subtleties, the nuances and the idiom are sometimes lost. The newspapers sometimes do not have a proper style sheet, which is supposed to be mandatory. We find a mix of UK English, American English and Indian English in the same report. This often applies to meanings as well as spellings. There are recurring instances of bad grammar, misspelling, incorrect punctuation, poorly constructed sentences, misused words, mixed metaphors, clichés, jargon, circumlocution etc.

CHAPTER 1

Print Media

Introduction

> Journalism: Its primary office is the gathering of news. At the peril of its soul it must see that the supply is not tainted. Neither in what it gives, nor in what it does not give, nor in the mode of presentation, must the unclouded face of truth suffer wrong. Comment is free but facts are sacred. (C.P. Scott, Editor and Proprietor, *Manchester Guardian*, 1922)

The writing style used in print media was different across periods in time. But, each newspaper has its own style of presenting the news. Be it the national dailies or the language press, each newspaper endeavours to create and establish its own signature style. But there are some guidelines to be followed to make writing for newspapers effective.

Initially, newspapers were allowed to print only the news, not comments or opinions as this was considered to be against the ethics of journalism. But this policy is no longer followed as newspapers do comment on political, social, sports and cultural events.

The language used in the print media is considered to be of a particular style. The purpose of a newspaper is to inform and the language used must succeed in communicating information sustaining the interest of the reader. As reporters are constrained by space they are forced to convey maximum information using minimum number of words. The system of language used has to serve the dual purpose of informing and entertaining the reader.

All newspapers carry different types of columns which demand specific styles of writing. We will first look at the basics of news writing.

News Stories

The term 'News' is a complex one and therefore cannot be given a narrow definition. It is an account of what is happening around us. It may involve details about current events, ongoing projects or plans for the future. News stories are written to inform the reader about a particular event or incident. There are certain factors to be considered while deciding whether a story is news worthy or not. They are:

Relevance

How relevant is a news story to the target audience? For example, an earthquake in India is not of much interest to readers in California. The closer an event takes place to the intended audience, the more important it is. This is why a big local or regional story might not make the national news.

Timeliness

When did it happen? Timing is extremely important in today's 24-hour news cycle. Recent events or events in the making are most likely to lead the news.

Importance, impact or consequence

How many people will the event impact? The greater the number the more important the story becomes.

Prominence

The actions of prominent people are much more likely to make the headlines. Politicians, entertainers and athletes are considered more newsworthy. If someone throws a shoe at another person, it is probably not news. If someone throws a shoe at the President of the United States, it will be in the news for weeks.

Predictability

Certain events such as elections, major sporting events and award announcements happen on a predictable schedule. As the event draws closer, it gains news value.

Continuity

Some events, such as war, elections, protests and strikes require continuing coverage. These events are likely to remain in the news for a long time, although not always as the lead story.

Human interest stories

Such stories always have a wide readership. For example, the story of a person overcoming great odds to reach his/her goal appeals to readers.

Negativity

Editors deem bad news more newsworthy than good news. Editors generally feel that conflict is more newsworthy than peace.

The unusual

Strange stories are likely to find their way into the news. 'Dog bites man' doesn't make a news story, whereas 'Man bites dog' definitely is newsworthy. But if the dog bites the president of the United States it is an international news story!

Structure of a News Story

Readers expect their newspapers to be accurate sources of information. A straight news story is supposed to be objective and fair. It is written in the structure of an 'inverted pyramid'. Following this structure, the 'base' of the pyramid – the most fundamental facts – appear at the top of the story, in the lead paragraph. Non-essential information appears in the following paragraphs, or 'nut graphs', in order of importance.

While some media writers are critical of the inverted pyramid structure, it remains one of the most widely used and time tested structures in mass media writing. The inverted pyramid structure also benefits editors. If an editor needs to cut an article, s/he can simply delete the details at the bottom.

In most news stories the essential facts of a story are included in the lead, the first sentence or two of the story. Good leads try to answer the 'five Ws and H' – who, what, when, where, why – and how as quickly as possible. Essential information generally refers to the 'Five Ws' of journalism: Who, What, When, Where and Why. The 'nut graphs' that follow contain additional details, quotes from sources, statistics, background or other information. These are added to the article in order of importance, so that the least important items are at the bottom.

A bare detail of facts is all that is needed when writing a news story. The writer does not give any comment or opinion. So this type of writing usually does not have an individual style or emotional colouring. The most important part of writing is organizing the text to create an impact on the reader. If you are writing about an event that has already been relayed through other medium, the way you organize your ideas and the linguistic (grammar and vocabulary) choices you make play a very important role in making the reader interested in your news story.

Linking Ideas

Linking ideas through well-designed paragraphs make your news story very clear and interesting. The two distinct elements to paragraph organization are The **Topic sentence** (or clause) and **Supporting sentences**. The **Topic Sentence** expresses in general the point being made by the writer. It is often the first sentence of the paragraph. But sometimes there are exceptions. The supporting sentences then defend or argue the claim made by the topic sentence.

In the example below, you can identify the **Topic sentence**, which is in bold, and makes a general, rather abstract, claim. This is then supported by the simple statements of facts. But the **Supporting statements** not only justify the claim but also make the reader curious to read further to explore *the crisis the company is in*...the severity of the news.

Murthy returns to shore up Infosys. Bangalore: IT major Infosys announced that its Board at a meeting on Saturday morning re-appointed the company founder N.R. Narayana Murthy Chairman, pulling the 66-year old IT services pioneer out of his two-year retirement. While desisting to comment on the crisis the company is in, Mr. Murthy maintained that his role would only be "value add" to the current leadership. (*The Hindu*)

Let us list the various ways in which a paragraph can develop the support of the **Topic sentences**.

Using...

1. Simple statements of facts;
2. Illustrative incidents;
3. Figures and statistics;
4. Logical arguments and
5. Direct or indirect quotes.

Analyse

Look at the paragraph below and identify both the topic sentence and the type of support given.

Infant Deaths Shatter Attappady

Four deaths reported in last 3 days taking the toll to 52 in last 16 months

Palakkad: The death of tribal infants does not seem to end in Attappady as four deaths were reported in the last three days taking the toll to 52 in to the last 16 months.

On Saturday, the child of Pushpa and Murugan of Cheerakadavu tribal hamlet of Pudur Gramapanchayat died at a private hospital in Coimbatore. The delivery was on Friday.

On Thursday night, the child of Sarada and Durai of Melemully in Pudur Gramapanchayat died soon after birth at the Kottathara Tribal Speciality Hospital. Sarada had been shifted to the Palakkad District Hospital as she suffered from High Blood Pressure.

These incidents show the failure of the government in taking preventive steps to bring the death of infants under control, said Rajendra Prasad, president of Thampu as an organisation working for the tribal people.

An eight-member Central Team which is at Attappady from May 20 to study the death of infants, had found that pregnant women and adolescent girls suffered from malnutrition. Steps should be taken for the safety of expectant women and adolescent girls, the team members felt.

The central government also found that the nutritious food had not been distributed to the children and the pregnant women there through the Anganwadis in the last two years.

Schemes of the central government such as Safala and Indira Gandhi Matru Yojana had not been implemented in the last two years. (*The Hindu*)

Research

1. How are the paragraphs developed?
2. Do they always start with the topic sentence?
3. Is the relationship between the topic sentence and the rest of the paragraphs clear?
4. How does the structure of the paragraph influence the reading of the text?

The use of linking phrases like **such as** indicates that the information that follows serves the same rhetorical function as the information that precedes it.

Discussion:

Look at the Discourse Linkers Below:

Moreover, above all, in addition
On the contrary, in that case, therefore
But, so, that, and
That is to say, in any case, by contrast
On the other hand, indeed, whereas
Furthermore, while, because
However, nevertheless, although.

Within the categories arranged discuss whether it is possible to replace one of the linking words with another without changing the meaning. (Could you replace 'However' with 'On the contrary'?)

The Passive

Writers often use the passive voice as this makes the report more formal and also positions the object of the verb at the head of the sentence.

Can you identify the passives used in the paragraph above? Passives are very easy to locate if you know the meaning. The form is 'to be +past participle' like: **is, are, am, were, has been, have been, had been, will be, will have been or being followed by a past participle**. Using the passive is really a matter of choice. If the subject or agent of an action is not relevant to the context, we use passive.

For example, ***Five arrested in Mumbai Blast Case*** *and* ***Police arrested Five People in the Mumbai Blast Case*** have the same meaning.

But by using the passive voice the writer is focussing on the result of the action as the doers of this action is implied. News reports often use the passive voice to remain neutral.

The passive is also used to distance/distinguish the writers' personal viewpoint from that s/he is expressing.

For example, ***It is often argued that cancer has become a lifestyle disease.***

Task

Look at the following sentences. Discuss how the variation in thematic foregrounding influences the meaning.

The cost of construction was agreed on.
The cost of construction was agreed on by the builders.
They agreed on the cost of construction.
The builders agreed on the cost of construction.

The writer has to take care to keep the **vocabulary** neutral. Adjectives have to be judiciously used. It is a narration of events with the latest development at the top.

Using **synonyms** in a news report keeps it interesting. As a lot of information is conveyed in a very short space, it is important that the listener pays attention. If we hear the same word being repeated we might get bored and stop reading further. By using **synonyms or near-synonyms** the writer can sustain the reader's interest.

The writer has to verify the facts and if they are not completely confirmed s/he has to use words with extreme care.

For example, *It is alleged that Mr Patel committed the crime.* Here it becomes very clear that it is not a confirmed fact that Mr Patel is guilty but that there is a shadow of doubt regarding his involvement in the crime.

Be clear about the difference in meaning of the words 'accused' and 'alleged'. It is only after legal charges have been filed against a person that you can refer to him as the accused.

Mr Joseph was said to have opposed the proposal.

The writer has to be vigilant about choosing the right words as well as the correct syntactic structure to convey the lack of affirmative facts or evidence.

As the writer is writing against the constraints of space vocabulary has to be used judiciously. There are certain words that are commonly found in newspapers. Some of them are:

- **Political and economic terms:** *Stability, electioneering, opinion polls, human rights, terrorist network, budget deficit, devalued currency etc.*
- **Emotionally coloured terms:** Words that are used in specialized ways to convey ideas. For example, the use of the verb ***to dog*** means *to follow* as in 'Photographers *dogged* the princess all her adult life'.
- **Strong adjectives and metaphors:** These are used to convey the impact of the news item. ***War hysteria, war mongering, sweeping majority, a storm of applause, boardroom battles, noisy protests escalating prices.***
- **Clichés:** These are hackneyed, stereotyped expressions generally considered to be a defect in writing. But they are necessary in newspaper writing as the readers are familiar with these expressions and so they prompt the correct associations of ideas thereby preventing ambiguity that leads to misunderstanding. For example, ***long-term agreements, a melting pot, crucial/pressing problems, zero tolerance, political correctness***, etc.
- **Abbreviations:** Newspapers make full use of abbreviations as they save space. Names of organizations, public and state bodies, political associations, companies, various offices known by their initials are very common; e.g., ***EU, UNO, WTO,*** **DMRC,** etc.
- **Neologism:** It is generally defined as 'a new word or a new meaning for an established word'. Newspapers are quick to react to any new development, hence new words make their way into the language of the newspaper quite often. For example, ***cyber-intrusions, eco-commercial,*** **biologically *engineered, genetically modified*** etc.
- **Foreign words:** These are borrowed words from different languages such as ***Ad-hoc*** **[(specialized; from Latin);** ***bona fide*** **(real; from Latin)].**

Indigenous (Desi) words in English Newspapers in India

> It has often been noticed that the mother tongue creeps into English language in many newspapers. Though this might be confusing for a person who does not know the language some insist that this keeps the writing racy. "Hinglish (Hindi and English) boasts of 'air-dashing' to a crisis (famine or fire) lest newspapers accuse them of 'being on the back foot'. Hinglish is a dialect pulsating with energy and invention that captures the essential fluidity of Indian society.
> (Deep K Datta-Ray, Tryst With Modernity. *The Times of India*, 18 August 2010)

Writing the Headline

Headlines have to contain a clear, succinct and if possible, intriguing message to interest the reader, who is usually a person whose eye moves swiftly down a page and stops when something catches his/her attention. The headline of a news story is the short summary which introduces the story. The best way to write a good headline is to keep it simple and direct. Headlines should not be full, complete sentences, but short summaries that will attract attention.

Tips on writing headlines

- If possible use a verb. It denotes action and makes the sentence powerful.
- Use the active voice. Passive voice is more formal and may require more words.
- Use present tense to convey the sense that the event just happened.
- Avoid ambiguity.
- Do not capitalize every word.
- Avoid repeating words.
- Draw on idioms – identify phrases or expressions associated with the story's theme.

- Use of punctuations: The 'period' or 'full stop' is not used at the end of the headline. It may be only used in abbreviations to make them more understandable. For example, Govt. losing money every year. Comma is used as a substitute for 'and' in order to save space. It is also used to separate two clauses. For example, *Salaries of CM, Speaker, MLAs hiked.*
- Use puns judiciously. If it is a serious story it is better not to use puns. Use plays-on words to contribute to meaning in lighter news stories.
- Don't repeat the lead in the headline.

Some words are omitted to make the headline catchy. The words which are usually omitted include:

- **Articles.**
  President declares celebration
  The president has declared **a** celebration.
- **Auxiliary verbs:**
  Kochi Metro hit by hitch
  The Kochi Metro **has been** hit by a hitch
- **Possessive adjectives:**
  Chidambaram pins hopes on Supreme Court
  Chidambaram has pinned **his** hopes on the Supreme Court.

Effective headlines usually involve logical sentence structure, active voice and strong present-tense verbs. Always remember that your headline has to fit the allocated space. The first word in the head should be capitalized as should all proper nouns. Most headline words appear in lower-case letters.

Exercise:

Write **Headlines** for the following news stories:

1. A man said to have Chechnya links was shot dead by law enforcement officers while being questioned in connection with the April 15 Boston Marathon bombing, the FBI has confirmed.

2. The BSE benchmark Sensex on Thursday fell for the fourth consecutive day by losing nearly 85 points in early trade due to sustained selling by funds amid a weak trend in other Asian markets.
3. The usually laidback morning hours at the court complex were replaced by a 'peaceful, non-violent open air jam' to support Irom Sharmila Chanu at her next Delhi trial. A Mumbai-based rapper and an alternative jazz duo accompanied by students and trade unionists gathered on the lawns of the Patiala House Courts Complex early on Wednesday.
4. Social activist Medha Patkar met residents affected by the Chennai airport expansion project here in Manapakkam on Wednesday. After meeting the residents, she told media-persons that the State government must denotify the lands acquired from the residents for the expansion work, since Airport Authority of India (AAI) had said that some of the allotted land might not be needed.
(*The Hindu*)

Writing the Lead

The lead, or opening paragraph, is the most important part of a news story. It gives readers the most important information in a clear, concise and interesting manner. It also establishes the voice and direction of an article. The type of story determines whether the lead will be hard or soft. A hard lead tells the audience the vital details of the story immediately. Hard leads are usually used for breaking news.

At least 30 people were injured in the collapse of the building.

A soft lead takes a more subtle approach; it alerts the audience to the news that is to follow. This approach is sometimes called 'warming up' the audience. Soft leads may not be as dramatic as hard leads, but they do invite the audience to continue reading.

Before writing a lead, decide which aspect of the story – **who, what, when, where, why or how** – is most important. Then try to give answers to all the questions that may arise in the minds of the readers.

Examples:

Two rebels of the banned XYZ were killed in an encounter with police in Kashmir on Thursday.

This lead has enumerated the 'what', 'where', 'when' and 'how' elements very clearly. ***Forest Minister M.G. Kumar today made an appeal to the members of the State Assembly to contribute Rs. 2 lakhs from their funds for forest conservation programmes in their constituencies.***

In this lead the elements of 'who', 'what' and 'where' have been explained. Some other points that are to be considered while writing the lead are:

Specificity: Though you are essentially summarizing information in most leads, try to be specific as possible.

Example:

Former Prime Minister Nawaz Sharif's Pakistan Muslim League-Nawaz established an unbridgeable lead over other parties in Saturday's elections. Imran Khan's Pakistan Tehreek-e-Insaf and the Pakistan People's Party were in a neck-and-neck tussle for a distant second position with leads in 37 seats each.

(*The Hindu*)

The reporter has conveyed the most important information answering most of the questions likely to rise in the reader's mind.

Brevity: Readers want to know why a story is important and you have to tell them that in as few words as possible. Avoid unintentional redundancy. Go right to the heart of the story. Many writers make the mistake of overusing adverbs and adjectives in their leads. Concentrate instead on using strong verbs and nouns.

Example: ***Sixteen-year-old Chingkheinganba Nameirakpam is the youngest climber of Mount Everest from the north-east. He scaled the highest peak at 5 am on Saturday.***

The writer has given the relevant details using less than 30 words.

Active sentences: Strong verbs will make your lead lively and interesting. Passive constructions, on the other hand, may sound dull.

Honesty: A lead is an implicit promise to your readers. You must be able to convey all the details that you mentioned in your lead.

Types of Leads

Summary lead: This is the most traditional lead in news writing. Straight news leads tend to provide answers to the most important three or four of the five W's and H. Decide what needs to be answered first and provide information accordingly.

Example: Twenty-eight passengers and a crew of four were killed last night when an Air India flight to Dubai crashed immediately after takeoff from Delhi.

Anecdotal lead: Sometimes, beginning a story with a quick anecdote can capture the attention of the readers. The anecdote must be interesting and must closely illustrate the article's main point. Usually, such anecdotal or narrative leads are used in features. If you use this approach, specificity and concrete details are essential, and the broader significance of the anecdote should be clarified in the first few sentences that follow the lead.

Example: **Anju vividly remembered the day her father sold her.** She was 13. It was during the rainy season of 1999. Two men came to her village in the eastern hills of Nepal. They said they would give her work in Kathmandu. But she was trafficked across the border to India, where she was forced to work as a prostitute in the red-light district of Mumbai for four years.

Question lead: This can be useful in grabbing attention, but the editors do not usually prefer this lead as it is not as effective as other types of leads in providing the main point of a story. In this case, the second paragraph must carry a lot of the weight that would normally be handled in the lead. The question lead features a pertinent query that arouses the readers' curiosity and makes them want to go on reading for the answers. Make sure the question is rhetorical and cannot be answered with a straight 'no' or 'yes'.

Example: Are you tired of hormones as cultural myth, as shorthand for swagger and machismo, ferocity and obnoxiousness, the bearskin beneath the three-piece suit? (*The Times*)

The Contrast Lead: This highlights conflicts or difference. It is used for stories about disagreements or unusual circumstances.

Example: Boston will never be the same. This is a place, after all, where terrorists don't venture. But Monday changed everything. Two powerful bombs exploded near the finish line of the Boston Marathon on Monday afternoon, killing three people, including an 8-year-old child, and injuring more than 100, as one of this city's most cherished rites of spring was transformed from a scene of cheers and sweaty triumph to one of screams and carnage (*New York Times*)

Teaser Lead: It teases the imagination or withholds information to provoke the reader's curiosity.

Example: On Wednesday, Lieutenant Commander Abhilash Tomy had a hard time at the Immigration Office at Yellow Gate police station to get his passport stamped. He tried convincing them about Sagar Parikrama II. **"I am going around the world in a boat, alone," he told them.**

(*The Hindu*)

Quotation Lead: The quotation must be directly related to the topic. Be sure to put it within quotation marks and give credit to the person who said it.

Example: **'No differences with JD(U)'**, said Jaitley after the party meeting held today in Delhi. (*The Hindu*)

Exercise

1. Identify the type of lead used:
   (a) Another round of power tariff hike is in the offing, this time to raise revenue in excess of 40 per cent of the existing income as the distribution companies submitted proposals to the A.P. Electricity Regulatory Commission (APERC) for permission to raise Rs. 12,723 crore additionally from consumers. (*The Hindu*)
   (b) Separate buses for schoolboys and schoolgirls, overcoats for girls, ban on mobile phones on campuses and restricted interaction of girls and boys – these are the steps the Puducherry government has decided on to enforce to prevent harassment

of girl students. Squads would be formed to check use of mobile phones by students, Secretary of Education G. Ragesh Chandra told *The Hindu*. (*The Hindu*)

(c) The stage had visibly shrunk. There was no DMK, no TMC and no surprise last minute entry by Samajwadi chieftain Mulayam Singh Yadav, to applaud UPA-II's fourth 'Report to People'. (*The New Indian Express*)

2. Write a delayed lead for a news story on rise of diesel prices in the country.

Body Paragraphs

These are the questions that you need to ask yourself before you start writing your article.

1. What is my most important information?
   The most important information usually goes into the lead paragraph.
2. What other pieces of information are essential to relay the information to the reader?
3. What information can be omitted in this article without compromising on the relevant details?

- Inverted pyramid – The summary lead appears first and then information is presented in descending order of importance.

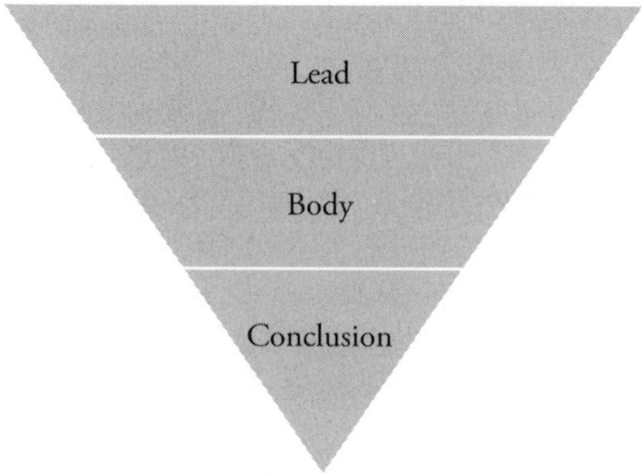

- **Hour glass style** starts with an inverted pyramid, then has 'the turn' which moves the story into a chronological conclusion.
  Inverted Pyramid
  The Turn
  A Chronological Narration
- **The focus style** begins with an anecdotal or narrative lead that is used to illustrate a larger problem. It has a circle ending, which means that the conclusion alludes to the lead.

The body paragraphs support the lead and nut graphs, with suitable quotes, facts, anecdotes, explanations and points of view. The main point of a paragraph is known as **the *controlling idea.***

Body paragraphs will begin with an explanation of the controlling idea; this is the topic sentence. The rest of the paragraph supports that topic sentence, by explaining it in detail, giving an example or citing evidence that reinforces it.

The subsequent paragraphs develop the facts mentioned in the lead and support the newsworthiness of the story. Cohesive devices are the links between sentences and paragraphs which enable the reader to understand the article as a whole. Cohesion can be achieved in the following ways.

- ***Repetition of vocabulary, or use of synonyms or general names to refer to the same object.***
  Example: An elephant was injured yesterday when it was run over by a bus. The pachyderm was being taken to a nearby temple.
- ***Use of articles to indicate known information***
  Example: A woman who fell 10 metres from a hill was lifted to safety by a helicopter. The woman fell while climbing.
- Variations in word order to put old information towards the beginning of sentences and new information towards the end. This often requires structures such as passive voice to change the normal word order of subject-verb-object.
- Use of linking words such as conjunctions, prepositions and adverbs.

Body paragraphs do not exist in isolation. One must flow into the next. Transitions in thought must be reflected in the writing using suitable cue words. Transitions show the connections between paragraphs themselves and the connections between the paragraphs and the overall focus of the article. Transitions maintain the apt momentum in your essay and ensures readability.

Examples: earlier, later, before, after, promptly and tardy.

Exercise

1. The IPL match fixing
2. The Boston massacre
3. A train tragedy that kills 50 people
4. The Aranmula airport

Slant

Though journalists are advised to be neutral in their reporting it is often noticed that most newspapers have a political slant. It is not just reflective of the owners' political predilections. The bias is sometimes maintained to satisfy the target audience. Slant refers to the mode of presenting information in such a way that it appeals to certain groups in society. Bias has almost the same meaning as slant, but has strong negative connotations. Journalism can never be completely objective and neutral: there will always have to be editorial choices about what stories to include, how to approach each story, which should be lead stories, the kind of vocabulary used the choice of photographs and so on.

- Corporate bias – sympathetic reporting of the interests of the owners of the newspaper sponsors/advertisers.
- Political bias – bias in favour of or against a particular political party.
- Religious and cultural bias.
- Bias in favour of the exceptional over the ordinary. A tendency to emphasize the new and the different over the status quo or existing consensus.

An important aspect of slant is the use of different types of vocabulary to present certain information in either positive or negative light. Emotive vocabulary is used to make such points. For example, brutal attacker vs. brave fighter; tragic accident vs. unforgivable lapse and stubborn vs. tenacious.

- Bias by **omission** – To present the news story by leaving one point of view. To find instances of bias by omission, the reader has to be politically aware and check whether both sides have been given an opportunity to air their views.
- Bias by **selection of sources** – Sometimes newspapers tend to include more sources that support one view over another. Journalists look for quotes from eminent people to support their argument.
- The vocabulary used might contain phrases like; 'experts believe', 'observers say' or "most people believe". When a news story only presents one side, it is obviously the side the reporter supports.
- Bias by **story selection** – News stories that reflect well on certain political parties are highlighted whereas the involvement of the other side is downplayed.
- Bias by **placement** – Story placement indicates how important the editor considers the story. Bias by placement occurs depending on the space and placement allocated in the paper for an article or a story. It refers to a pattern of placing news stories so as to downplay information supportive of any particular political party.
- Bias by **labelling** – Tagging of certain politicians and groups with extreme labels giving others neutral or positive labels.
- Bias by **tone** – This occurs when the story has only one interpretation of an event or decision, to the exclusion of other points of view or perspectives.

The Editing Process

The reporter is the radar of the newspaper which is its outside surveillance mechanism, while the editor is the gatekeeper, a decision maker who decides what will be published and what should be rejected. The editor decides the format of the news story, its length and where it should appear on the newspaper. The main consideration in editing is to tell the story in the fewest words possible. Condensation should not affect clarity. Clarity can be ensured by avoiding complex sentence constructions and by using familiar expressions. Accuracy should not be compromised on.

Duties of an editor

1. Makes sure that the story conforms to the style of the newspaper.
2. Adjusts story length to space requirements.
3. Corrects factual errors
4. Makes stories objective and legally safe.
5. Checks for clarity and corrects language errors.
6. Substitutes jargon with words that are understood buy the common reader.
7. Guard against journalese. (Journalese is language used by journalists when they try to avoid using the obvious word and look for alternatives. But this causes ambiguity.)

Subbing

A sub-editor is a person who corrects and checks articles in a newspaper before they are printed.

A sub-editor is responsible for ensuring that the tone, style and layout of the final copy match the style followed by the publication house and also suit the target market. The work involves processing the entire copy before it is published, to ensure that it is grammatically and factually correct and that it reads well. Sub-editors also lay out the story on the page, write headings and may be involved with overall page design.

A sub-editor, thus, is responsible for giving the finishing touch to the to-be-published material. S/he turns the dry dull facts or information into interesting and readable one. She or he guards the newspaper world against the charges of libel, misrepresentation, silly grammatical and spelling errors and more. The sub editor must have good command over language and should be diplomatic.

Writing Editorials

One common feature found in all daily newspapers is the editorial page. The editor writes the analysis of major national and international news items. The editorial page reveals the newspaper's point of view. An editorial is a critical interpretation of significant, contemporary events to inform and influence the reader to assume a particular stance. It can be an opinion from any point of view, but has to be backed by sufficient facts. Editorials are meant to influence public opinion and encourage critical thinking. The editorial helps the reader to understand the implications of policies and decisions taken by the authorities. The writer must take into account the policy of the newspaper while taking a position on any issue. Mostly, editorials are written by senior editorial staff, but they are unsigned. The editorial becomes the personality of the newspaper. All editorials are interpretative and explanatory, while some might be controversial. Such editorials are prime examples of persuasive writing because they try to propagate a particular idea or policy by presenting only the negative features of the opposite side. Some newspapers run duelling editorials during elections with each side taking up for a particular side.

Writing an editorial demands a judicious choice of vocabulary. The language must be unambiguous and concise. The presentation of ideas must be logical, and the data must be analysed in detail. The basic difference between a news article and an editorial is the stance of the writer. In a news article as a writer, you are expected to cover the facts and be neutral in your writing; whereas in an editorial you can give your own opinion, based on various facts. After choosing a topic, you will have to take a stance. Decide whether you are against it or for it. You have to back your opinion with some strong facts. Vague opinions have no place in an editorial. In the introductory paragraph, you should put forth your opinion about the topic. You should also refute the claims you oppose. You can use statistical data or give examples from history to prove your point. When presenting arguments, make sure that you keep your strongest argument towards the end. The arguments in an editorial must be substantiated by factual evidence.

The opening paragraph of an editorial must invite the reader to read further. The writer must maintain the tempo and sustain the interest of the reader in the following paragraphs by providing concrete facts and quoting from credible sources.

The conclusion of your editorial should provide a brief summary of your opinion that is expressed in the article and at the same time either offer solutions or trigger the reader's thought process. The editorial must end with a strong closing appeal. The use of memorable and appealing words at the end of an editorial exhorts your audience to take action.

The length of your editorial will depend on the topic you choose and what you have to say about it. There is no stipulated limit on the length of the editorial. Generally, well-written editorials are the ones with ample facts to support the writer's view. Length is by no means the determinant of a good editorial. Some of the best editorials are concise, yet successful in making a strong point.

Don't use bombastic or opaque language to convey your ideas. Keep the language simple and direct. Make use of repetition. Salient points in the editorial must be re-echoed to ensure that the reader is at home with the message.

Op-ed Pieces

An op-ed, abbreviated from opposite the editorial page, is a newspaper article that expresses the opinions of a writer who is usually unaffiliated with the newspaper's editorial board. These are different from editorials, which are usually unsigned and written by editorial board members. They run from 850 to 1000 words. Newspapers allot space for free for op-ed articles and letters to the editor as part of their commitment to the public.

Letters to the Editor

It is through writing letters to the editor that the readers express their opinions. Letters for publication should be brief, must refer to an article that has appeared within the last seven days and must include the writer's address and phone number. The letters published in the newspapers are representative in nature; it usually reflects the opinion of a number of readers.

Feature Writing

A feature story is different from a news story in one respect – its intent. A news story provides information about an event, idea or situation. The feature does something more – it may also interpret news and add depth to a story with an intention to instruct or entertain the readers. A news feature explores a story. It has the freedom to be less time sensitive than news stories. A feature is longer than an ordinary news story.

- A feature takes an in–depth look at what happens behind the scenes.
- It tries to explain how and why a particular trend developed.
- A feature may be written based on the profile of a person or a group.
- A feature adopts a particular angle and explores a story from that angle. There are different ways by which you can identify the angle you wish to adopt. You will also need marshal your thoughts, mentally classify and catalogue the information you have gathered. Only then can you get some semblance of perspective or the **angle** you will use. Sometimes the angle will reveal itself through the gathering and reviewing of information.
- Sometimes, you will need to write conforming to a particular brief. For example, if you are commissioned to write a piece, then that will dictate the angle you adopt.

The first step to write a feature is research. The writer must gather information from a variety of sources. The writer interviews the people involved and attempts to draw conclusions from the information obtained. The writer must be careful to present a balanced view of the issue and, to ensure this, opinions of people who have opposing views on the topic should be recorded.

The structure

- **The headline** should be as catchy as possible because your reader will read this first then decide whether or not to read the story.

- The **introduction** is the most important part. It is your introduction that has to entice your reader. Use drama, emotion, quotations, questions and descriptions to make your introduction attractive.
- The **body** of the article needs to answer all the questions raised in the introduction.
- Try and maintain an '**atmosphere**' throughout the writing.
- While the introduction draws the reader in, the **conclusion** should be written to help the reader remember the story. Therefore, use a strong punch line to conclude.

Some points to keep in mind while writing features

- Focus on human interest – the feel and emotion you put into the article are crucial to the success of the feature.
- Be clear about why you are writing the article. Is it to inform, persuade, observe, evaluate, or evoke emotion?
- Accuracy is important.
- Keep your audience clearly in mind – what are their desires, what really matters to them etc.

Interviews for features

This usually needs to be in-depth and in person rather than over the phone – this enables you to add colour and detail. While taking the interviews:

- Ensure that every quote, fact and anecdote relates to your theme in some way.
- Decide on the '**tense**' of your story at the start and continue using it throughout the story unless the situation demands that you change the tense.
- Avoid lengthy, complex paragraphs. Your article will appear in columns, so one or two sentences make a paragraph.
- Write in the active voice. In active writing, people **do** things.

- Be careful about spelling and grammar and always check before you send the article for publication.
- Ideas come from everywhere – watch, read, listen, keep up-to-date and take notes. Talk to people in different fields to find out what interests and concerns them.

Exercise

Write a feature on:

1. Illegal sand mining in Kerala/UP.
2. Migrant labourers in Kerala.
3. New Generation Cinema.

Book Reviews

Newspapers usually have a panel of specialists who write book reviews for them. The reviewer must have in depth knowledge of the subject and should be able to assess the book in terms of its impact on the reader. The purpose of a review is to give an account of the book and offer a reasoned opinion about its qualities. The main task of the writer is to report on the content, the approach and the scope of the work for the benefit of the readers. The book review should contain a brief description of the book and a short account of the author. The book reviewer tells the reader whether a book is worth reading or not. Since the reviewer has the power to affect the sales of the book, the review should be unbiased. An ideal review should give an overview of the book to the readers and an evaluation based on the reviewers' taste and experience.

The opening paragraph should grab the attention of the reader. This passage can be conversational in tone. You can be slightly provocative. Its purpose is to introduce the work under review and to encourage the reader to read on.

The body of the review will be a series of short paragraphs – around fifty words each in length. The concluding paragraph can summarize the reviewer's opinion and may offer a personal comment which echoes the introduction. The total length of the review should be between 500 and 1,000 words. It may depend on the publication and how many columns are allotted for a book review.

Full bibliographic details of the work under review must be included. Be sure to state:

- The name of the author(s);
- Title and sub-title;
- Place of publication;
- Publisher;
- Date of publication;
- Number of pages and
- The full ISB number.

A very readable, informative, much loved column in *The Hindu* titled *Print Pick* introduces the new books. Listed below is the short review format of Khaled Hossein's *And the Mountains Echoed.* Look at the language used.

Crossing generations and continents, moving from Kabul, to Paris to San Francisco to the Greek island of Tinos, the author writes about the bonds that define us and shape our lives, how the choices we make resonate through history. (*The Hindu*, Monday June 3, 2013)

Exercise

Given below are some vocabulary and some phrases. Use any of them to write a short book review.

Clear, simple prose, startling candour, earthy sense, focusing on, gripping, odd twists and turns, intense, mediates, takes us on a journey, versatile, contemplative.

Film Reviews

Whenever a new movie is released, people look to film reviews to decide if they should see it. Movie reviews can make or break a film's box office collection. If you write a review for a newspaper, be honest about your opinion of the movie. Keep your word count in mind too. Your review should be specific and concise. When writing a review consider who the intended audience is for the film.

Steps

- The first step is to watch the movie.
- Make notes about your impressions of the movie.
- Be careful to maintain your objectivity.
- Don't be swayed by your preference or dislike for the director or a particular actor starring in the movie.
- In the review specify the successful and unsuccessful elements in the movie.
- List the names of the director, actors and other pertinent information.
- The first paragraph should include the name of the film, its stars, setting and genre.
- Write a short plot summary in your second paragraph.
- Include the details that give your audience a brief glimpse of the film.
- Do not give away any plot twists or the climax.
- Discuss relevant parts of the movie.
- Include your opinion of the direction, script, actors and photography.
- A good film review uses scenes and dialogues to support its larger argument.
- Do not be too harsh in your criticism.

Interviews for Print

Conducting a good interview requires detailed planning and good communication skills. Plan ahead so that you use the interviewee's time wisely. Know as much as possible about the person before you sit down for the interview. Research in depth and speak to the people who are close to the subject. If you are planning a detailed interview it is better to ensure that the interviewee knows what to expect.

- Don't reveal all your questions at this stage as you may lose spontaneity.
- In certain situations you might have to give the list of questions beforehand.
- Plan out a rough list of what you want to ask.
- It shouldn't be a rigid script, because sometimes the person's answers will take you in an unexpected direction that is better than what you planned.
- Be sure to follow that direction and ask leading questions.
- Make sure that the interviewee is relaxed.
- You can start a casual conversation before you begin the actual interview.
- A relaxed subject will open up to you.
- Keep a comfortable level of eye contact with the subject.
- Let your facial expression be relaxed and your body's position convey interest.
- Remember that most people are either nervous or wary of being interviewed; they're putting a lot of trust in you by consenting to let you represent them in print. Try to put them at ease. Unless they feel comfortable and relaxed they will not talk freely to the interviewer.
- Try to ask the questions, even the difficult ones, in a sympathetic manner.

There are several types of questions:

Open questions: 'Wh' questions demand an elaborate answer.

Closed questions like yes/no questions, or those that start with auxiliary verbs, like Will you? Or do you? help you to get specific answers if you feel that the subject is being evasive.

Negative questions like Why didn't you? Or haven't you? are considered aggressive but they succeed in opening up controversial areas which makes a good copy.

Echo questions repeat the last part of the question. This elicits more information. For example, 'I never said that MR X is a liar'. 'Never'?

Don't rush to fill in the silences. Develop a repertoire of verbal and visual clues that indicate that you want the other person to elaborate. And when all else fails, you can continue to ask leading questions, like, ***'Can you tell me more about that?'***

Listening to what the other person is saying is only half the story. You have to be able to understand body language. Read the body language of the person you're interviewing and if you feel that they are becoming defensive, back away from the question you are asking and if possible come back to the question later.

Observe the persons' mannerisms, gestures, listen to the volume and steadiness of the voice, etc. and notice how he/she has dressed and groomed himself/herself and also the details of the surroundings.

Try to make your writing as unobtrusive as possible. If you let the interview remain conversational and pleasant, people often will relax and talk much more naturally. But remember to keep control of the interview; don't let the subject ramble or stray from the subject. Always remember that it is best that you record the interview. This is the evidence that cannot be denied. You have to tell the person that you are recording the conversation.

The next is when you reconstruct the interview by writing it putting together the observations and the recording. It is better to do it soon after the interview as it is fresh in your mind.

The Proust questionnaire is a questionnaire about one's personality. These questions were answered by the famous French writer Marcel Proust. These questions are supposed to reveal the personality of the subject and hence are often used for celebrity interviews.

Given below is an extract from an interview from **Proust questionnaire**. The celebrity is Padmashri Kadri Gopalnath who is synonymous with the Indian Classical Saxophone. Write a profile about him using the information that you get from the interview. Give a suitable title and check whether you chose the same title as the Interviewer.

1. What is your idea of happiness?
   I am happiest when I do not hurt anyone. When you try to make everyone around you happy, you too experience happiness.
2. What is your greatest fear?

There are a few fears that haunt me. I fear I may unwillingly cheat someone. I fear I lose my power to get rid of my ego. I fear that one day I may change.

3. Which living person do you most admire?
   My guruji T.V. Gopalakrishnan. What I most admire about him is his uncanny knack of spotting talent. He would go out of the way to promote and encourage this talent. He has helped so many young musicians to find their feet.
4. What is the trait you most deplore in yourself?
   Attempting to find perfection in everything.
5. What is the trait that you most deplore in others?
   Lack of respect for elders. This *bharathiya parampara* (Indian Tradition) is almost lost. It used to be customary for the young musicians to touch the feet of the elders. This I find is rapidly vanishing.
6. What is your greatest extravagance?
   Call it extravagance if you will, but I'm not stingy, when it comes to buying clothes, especially those I wear for concerts. On stage, I believe, an artist must look neat and presentable. Appearance is important.
7. What do you consider the most overrated virtue?
   Undue respect. I have felt awkward when people, especially elders touch my feet. I wonder whether I deserve this. And I pray I don't get carried away by such a show of affection.
8. What is the greatest love of your life?
   My music, my saxophone is the greatest love of my life.
9. What is your greatest regret?
   Not having my parents with me now.
10. When and where were you happiest?
    When I am at concert.

Linking ideas: Within sentences

When you read the profile that you have written based on the interview, you get an idea about the way we organize sentences contextually to bring clarity. You can identify the use of ***clause complex*** in the interview as well as in the profile that you have written. A more familiar term for this is more specifically – compound or complex sentence.

For example, I like Music and I like painting (**compound**).
She went to the library but couldn't find him (**complex**).

List a few sentences and decide what type of clauses they contain. Discuss how the conjunctions link ideas both between and within sentences.

For example,

1. I wonder whether I deserve it.
2. Before I begin my concert, I keep my mind clear, meditate and there is silence around.
3. Analyse how the conjunctions help the reader to understand the meaning.

Writing for Magazines: Action – Angle – Anecdote

Newspaper articles convey facts, but, magazine articles try to create an experience for their readers with descriptive vocabulary that evokes sensory images. Here the content is as important as the style.

The first question to ask is: who is the target audience? If you are a freelancer then do identify the type of publication that will publish your article. It is important to target a specific audience. You should study the magazines you plan to write for and know exactly whom you are writing for.

- Choose a topic that you can cover with depth, detail and insight.
- After deciding the topic you have to do a lot of research.
- The next step is to work out which angle or perspective you will be writing the story from.
- Work out an angle; read at least a dozen articles on similar topics.
- See what has not been written on it. Try to create your own perspective. Many magazine stories lend themselves to the 'how' or 'why' angles.

- Tell the readers where and when your story is happening.
- Avoid an article in the first person unless you have a clear reason to do so. The only compelling reason to use this angle is that your experience offers fresh insight to the topic.
- Weave the story around one central idea or main theme.
- You will have a target length for your article. This word count will define your story structure.

The first step in the writing is to create a motivating opening story. The opening has to propel the reader into reading the rest of the article. The lead in a magazine article consists of the first two or three paragraphs. Its purpose is to:

- grab the reader's attention and
- tell the reader what the article is about.

The best type of magazine lead is the anecdote, which tells a story and portrays the larger theme. Immediately after the lead, write the main ideas in the article. Magazine writers call this the 'billboard paragraph' while newspaper writers call this the 'nut graph'.

Be clear about what you intend to say in the article. Write simple sentences with active voice, action verbs and strong nouns. Whenever you can replace an abstract concept with a specific word, do so. Anecdotes, examples and quotes are one way of providing concrete images. Try to paint a picture with words that stimulate an image in the reader's mind. For example, if you're writing about unemployment, write about the student who had to drop out of college because his father lost his job.

Organize related ideas and sentences close to one another and create smooth transitions. For example, you might start out with the 'what' aspect, go on to the 'how' aspect and finally focus on 'why' in the body of your story. The structure of a magazine article can follow the chronological format (past-present-future) or the flashback format (the article may start by referring to the past and then about the present and in the conclusion make predictions about the future). Direct quotes animate your article and attract and sustain the readers' attention.

If you are writing a magazine article based on a personal experience, you will need to write the story. Your story requires an incident, complications, conflict or obstacles, a climax and resolution. You must use the techniques of fiction, in particular the scene-building technique. A scene includes the following elements:

- Specific time and place;
- Action;
- Dialogue;
- Sensory images and
- Specific details.

You will want to make your readers aware of the time and place. This is your setting. You will need to use language that appeals to the reader's sense of smell, taste, sight and touch. A good scene also includes vivid descriptions that helps the reader visualize the story. In the conclusion, you can write about the insight, understanding or lesson that you learned from the experience.

After writing make it a point to read your article carefully. Try to look at your writing through objective and impersonal eyes. Consider the purpose of your article. Was it to motivate readers to action? Did it achieve its purpose? Check for spelling and grammar carefully. The magazine has to be published on time so the writer has to take the responsibility to submit the articles before the deadline.

Techniques of editing

Editing should ensure accuracy, clarity and consistency. Try to read the story aloud. This will help you to check if the sentences are too long or complex. Check for inconsistencies in style. The style should be the same throughout the story. The story should not leave any unanswered questions in the reader's mind. Ensure that the article is unbiased and just.

Proofreading

When writing something important, such as a news story, it is important to check your work thoroughly for mistakes. This is called proofreading. Proofreading gives you a chance to make sure that no words are missing and that your spelling is correct. It is also a good idea to check that capital letters and punctuations such as question marks, apostrophes, commas and full stops are all in the right place.

Hints for successful proofreading

- Cultivate a sense of doubt while reading. There are certain types of common errors; double check for those.
- Read very slowly.
- Read what is actually on the page and not what you think is there.
- You have to deliberately slow down when you proof-read. The reason for deliberately slowing down is that when you read normally, you often see only the shells of words – the first and last few letters, perhaps.
- 'Fix your eyes' on almost every word in order to proofread accurately.
- You have to look at the word, not slide over it.
- In proofreading, you can take nothing for granted, because unconscious mistakes are very easy to make. It is beneficial to read out loud, because, you are forced to slow down.
- If possible, read aloud. You hear what you are reading as well as seeing it, so you are using two senses.
- It is often possible to hear a mistake, such as an omitted or repeated word that you have not seen while reading silently.

CHAPTER 2

Radio

Introduction

The radio is a mass medium that has enjoyed popularity since the 1930s. Though a medium that is only auditory in nature, it has managed, since its inception, to capture the imagination of people across the globe and remain competitive despite the entry of the visual and electronic media. It has held firm to its traditional role even while emerging in new avatars (internet radio and satellite radio). Perhaps, it is its ability to transform itself and cater to new audiences that makes it relevant in this day and age.

Radio Script

As with other scripts, radio scripts too are detailed and include all sounds that will be heard over the waves. The radio uses a two–column script. The left-hand column is narrower and includes the names of the speakers/characters and will indicate whether it is the announcer(s) who speaks or a character. The names are given in a vertical sequence in the order that they speak, in CAPS and followed by a colon. Any sounds (also known as effects or FX) and music that is to be incorporated into the programme is indicated in the script. All directions and instructions are given in CAPS and underlined. The details of music, direction etc. is given in the column on the right. The right-hand column is a wider column and contains dialogues or text spoken by the presenter/DJ/character.

Though the basic format of radio script remains unchanged and the two-column script is used, the structure, language, sound effects, tone and style differ based on the programme for which the script is written. Leave margins on all four sides of the page. The text should be indented.

Radio scripts are generally typed in double space, easy-to-read font and font size. Except for the dialogues, everything else such as instructions, indicators and cues etc. are typed in CAPS. This helps distinguish between dialogues and other information. In general, a one-page script translates into 90 seconds of speech. When writing radio scripts for news, ensure that each separate bit of news is included on a separate paper. In case the news does not fit on a single A4 size paper, indicate 'MORE' on the lower right hand side of the page. This will cue the news reader to the fact that the news does not end on the first page; rather it continues on the next page. When moving on to the next piece of news, start on a fresh sheet of paper. This helps avoid confusion and enhances readability.

SCENE 1	
SFX:	FOOTSTEPS RUSHING TOWARDS THE DOOR. DOOR OPENS. SOMEONE ENTERS. SOUNDS OF SEARCHING
BILL:	I know I left it here!! Where..is…it? PAPER RUSTLING Ohhh..please let me find it.. SOMEONE AT THE DOOR
ROBERTO:	(THREATENING) Found it?

Techniques of Writing for the Broadcast Media

Brevity is a key factor to keep in mind while writing a script for the radio. In print media, it is possible to use long sentences with complex structures to get a message across. This is because the reader can go back and re-read sentences if the meaning is unclear. The radio does not offer such a luxury. The listener has to get the message the first around. In order to do so, the script writer and/or the radio presenter has to ensure that short sentences are used – the kind of sentences that you would use in real-life conversations. The use of relative clauses is also not recommended.

As radio is a 'now' medium, the generally prescribed tense to be used is the present tense. There are two reasons for doing so. The present tense places the news or event in context – that it is happening at that point in time. It also implies immediacy or generates a sense of excitement that the listener is hearing the news as it unfolds.

Though the **past tense** may be used when appropriate it is normal to use **present tense**, especially in news, live programmes, chat and other programmes that take place in real-time or are recorded but meant to appear as though it takes place live. When talking about an event that took place in the past (which maybe a few hours ago/the previous night/a decade ago), past tense must be used so that the listener is able to place the event in the correct time frame.

Examples

- In an unexpected move, the US Senate declared its intention to impose trade sanctions on China last night.
- Political parties and human rights activists demanded a judicial probe into the custodial death of accused.
- He said China had appointed the former Foreign Minister and top diplomat Yang Jiechi as the new SR.
- Manchester United confirmed, on Thursday, that David Moyes would succeed Sir Alex Ferguson as manager of the club.

While writing a radio copy, keep the following points in mind:

- Write the way you speak.
- Use simple, everyday language, without being colloquial. (*The agreement has been called off* instead of *The agreement stands cancelled.* Or *Wait up! Where is the hurry?*)
- Meaning should be clear.
- Write in a way that creates immediate impact. (*President Obama pledged the full resources of the U.S. government to assist the tornado-hit community*).
- Progression of facts must be logical.
- It must be intrusive without being offensive.
- Sensitive portrayal of subjects and use of words should be maintained. (*Nearly 15 died and 20 were injured today in the bomb blast that occurred at the crowded Naya Ganj. The attack left the city reeling from its second attack in two weeks*).
- If the element of humour cannot be used in a copy, then use drama.
- Use easy to pronounce and familiar names for characters in play.
- Omit unnecessary words.
- Use descriptive language; use active voice and words and use more verbs than adjectives.

Football is arguably Britain's most successful ever export. But in giving it to others, the British lost control of the game they had created and crafted.
I've come to North London and I am high in the stands looking down onto a pitch that could honestly be used for playing Billiards. It's been mown into big wide strips and its currently being sprayed with water from the big water guns. This is the Emirates, home to the Arsenal Club...

(Source: BBC Radio4. *Sport and the British – Beating Us at Our Own Game*)

- Use music as a sound effect where appropriate.
- Use familiar sounds to help the narrative or dialogue create a visual image.
- Allow enough time to set a scene and establish a premise.

The words that you use and how they are used convey both meaning and emotion to listeners. Writing for radio broadcast demands that you 'speak' directly into the minds of the listener so that communication take place not through the gift of sight but that of sound.

A good writer must:

- Incorporate a medley of spoken words, sounds, special effects and music to make up for the lack of visuals.
- Paint pictures through these sounds and help set the scene and tone of the programme.
- Use music to add depth to content.
- Come up with an eloquent and striking beginning called **lead**.
- Write a **body** that fully explores the subject without shifting away from the focus.
- The **conclusion** must summarize the highlights.

Key Elements in Radio Jockeying

Elements that contribute to the overall listening experience are Voice, Diction, Delivery and Language.

As radio is a completely **audio-based medium**; the listeners are tuned to the smallest nuances of speech. The words, content, context, delivery – all make or add to the overall experience.

A good voice is an essential asset for a radio presenter. No one wants to listen to a voice that is harsh and grates on the nerves. The voice has to be clear, pleasant and easy on the ears. It is a powerful tool that can persuade and influence listeners. The presenter must have a warm and inviting voice that feels 'credible' and invites trust. At the same time you want to listen to a voice that is full of life and vitality. If you have a good voice you can do much to develop the gift but there is no real substitute for a good voice.

Along with voice, **diction** or the way the words sound, the stress that you place on words, is equally important. Diction contributes to clarity of speech and allows listeners to quickly grasp what is being said. It contributes to the overall impact of the text/message. Correct diction also allows the listener to concentrate on the important facts. Note how the meaning changes with change in diction.

> ***I*** hope to visit the Ontario Art Gallery. (I, as opposed to someone else, hope to visit the Gallery.)
> I ***hope*** to visit the Ontario Art Gallery. (Communicates uncertainty)
> I hope to visit the ***Ontario Art Gallery***. (Not someplace else.)

The manner of delivery also contributes to this. How a message is delivered (i.e., the tone) and the pace of delivery affects reception. An interactive manner of delivery or a friendly and humorous approach usually appeals to the audience. The manner of delivery is also determined by the programme/content that is being presented. The delivery of news differs from the delivery of a phone-in programme. One requires a brisk, matter-of-fact approach while the other calls for a warm, friendly and interested manner. Thus, delivery affects the image of a programme and determines how it is received.

Language is an important component in presenting news and the radio presenter has to adjust his/her language to suit the audience. The type of language used determines the mood and sets the tone of the programme. Language could be formal or informal. The language that you choose to use is determined by the kind of programme that you host/deliver as a radio presenter and your target audience. The language used in the news script follows a fixed pattern and is formal, matter-of-fact and devoid of words that imply subjectivity or communicate personal opinions/views. At the same time, when presenting a programme like a chat show or programme with comic high tones or a phone-in programme, the language used is informal, light and aims at being entertaining. The presenter uses colloquial and familiar words.

Note the vocabulary and grammatical inaccuracies in the script of *Atching Tan – A Gypsy Wife*. It contributes to the communication of information, places the story in context and enhances believability.

> 1: EXT. NELIUS AND LOVVIE'S PLOT. DAY:
> IT'S SUNDAY MORNING ON LONG SUMMER TRAVELLER'S SITE AND EVERYONE IS HOME. DOGS BARK, CHILDREN SHOUT AND PLAY.

NELIUS IS MENDING A CAR TYRE PUNCTURE. HE HITS THE IRON TYRE LEVER WITH A HAMMER SEVERAL TIMES. LOVVIE CALLS FROM THE OPEN TRAILER DOOR.

LOVVIE: Want a drink Nelius?

HE STOPS WORK

NELIUS: (OUT OF BREATH) Hey…?

LOVVIE: Juice or something?

NELIUS: Yeah… go on then.

HE HITS THE TYRE LEVER AGAIN WITH THE HAMMER.

NELIUS: And next time be careful where you're driving.

LOVVIE: That's a slow puncture divvie. Said yourself the tube ain't got a nail in or nothing.

NELIUS: Slow puncture's gotta start somehow.

SOMEONE PUTS RAP MUSIC ON SEVERAL PLOTS AWAY – LOUD

NELIUS: Oh what?

LOVVIE STEPS OUT OF THE TRAILER AND WALKS TOWARD NELIUS

LOVVIE: That's Loopy Loo again. (SHOUTING ACROSS THE SITE) Turn that music down will ya!

NELIUS: Where's Hank William's when you need him.

LOVVIE: Puts mi teeth on edge.

QUEENIE CALLS FROM HER TRAILER AT THE BACK OF THE PLOT.

QUEENIE: What's all that row?

LOVVIE: You can guess can't ya?

QUEENIE APPROACHES

QUENNIE: Her again.

NELIUS: You alright, aunt Queen?

QUEENIE: Not with that machine gun music I ain't.

LOVVIE: What I was saying.

QUEENIE: You got any idea what they're rokkering about in them songs?

NELIUS: Not a word.

QUEENIE: Bet your life it'll be mullorin somebody or stuffing drugs up their noses.

[Available at: www.bbc.co.uk/writersroom/scripts/atching-tan-a-gypsy-wife]

Tenses

US imposes sanction on China – While headlines can be in the present tense, the time factor must not be hidden.

Example: Latest developments in Washington include sanctions being placed on China. The announcement, made last night, will place severe restrictions on Chinese trade.

Note: The text starts off in the present tense and leads the listener to the conclusion that the news just broke. Phrases like ***'latest developments'*** add to this impression. While this is a ploy that is usually employed, it is misleading. A switch in the tense takes place within the same body of text. 'Will place' is in the **future tense** and can be used to talk about consequence and the present tense 'places' can be a good substitute. As a norm, switching between tenses is avoided to save the listener from unnecessary confusion.

Let's take a look at a few examples of usage of tense in various situations:

Introducing the show

Hello, listeners/Hello, people/Hello (Mumbaikers/Kochites etc.). I'm Nisha and you have tuned into Music Junction.

It's 3 in the afternoon and you are with me Nisha listening to your favourite Music Junction.

(**Present tense and active voice**).

Introducing guests

Hey People!/Hey, guys! Today I've something special in store for you. I have a special guest here in the studio with me. He is a youth icon and a star. He has lead the Indian cricket team to victories and held India's name high. He is none other than Virat Kohli. Virat, welcome to the show. And let me tell you, we are very excited to have you here with us.

(**Present tense and active voice**).

Introducing features

A feature can take the form of an interview/talk show, a news analysis, discussion and so on. All the above mentioned types of features are introduced in the present tense. A historical feature or a biography of a leader would be in the **past tense** as it would refer to events that occurred in the past. A radio feature on Mahatma Gandhi might begin with the narrator's voice saying something along the lines of ***'It was the year 1869. A year that changed history. The year was a prelude of things to come. More significantly (importantly), it saw the birth of a great man, the father of our nation, Mahatma Gandhi'.***

Introducing news

Good morning and welcome to the news at 7. This is Nalini Srivastav. Onto the headlines.

Introducing different genres of music

Yo, you people! It's 8 and let's kick off this evening on a high note with Black Eyed Peas **Pump it Up.** ***This zinger is sure to pump up your blood. So, here's me, DJ R, pumping it out to you.***

(Song is Played)

That was Pump it Up *from Black Eyed Peas. Now let's groove to Akon's and T. Pain's* Bartender.

Topic Sentence

The topic sentence is generally the first sentence of a paragraph, though this is not strictly necessary. It is the sentence that communicates the major point/idea of the paragraph. It is the nut graph sentence. It serves two purposes – it tells us what the basic idea conveyed in the paragraph is and helps link one paragraph to another (and in sense one idea to another) thus providing transition.

None can deny that the 2011 inflation has had an immense impact on world economy (clearly indicates that the following text discusses the impact/consequences of the 2011 inflation on the world economy).

India's demands in Italian sailors' case have met with strong resistance from the Italian government. (Sets the tone of the article and hints at what is to follow).

Exercise: Create topic sentences from the given headline/copy

1. China ends stand-off, pulls out troops from Daulat Beg Oldi sector.
2. Nawaz Sharif's Pakistan Muslim League-Nawaz (PML-N) party pulls ahead of Imran Khan's Pakistan Tehreek-e-Insaf (PTI) and the Pakistan People's Party (PPP).
3. Manjima Chatterjee wins The Hindu MetroPlus Playwright Award 2013.
4. Gurgaon to get 200 more buses.
5. Serena, Sharapova set up finale at Madrid Open.
6. Anand crushes Topalov of Bulgaria in the Norway Chess 2013 super tournament.

Phrasal Verbs

Phrasal verbs can be used to convey much in a few words and to communicate ideas clearly and concisely. For instance:

Tune into (Listen to/Change to) FM Rocks for an evening full of entertainment! You'll find that it *lives up to* fans' expectations and leave you ***panting for*** more.

Hey, guys! You are ***hanging out with*** me, Andre.

Put on your dancing shoes and groove to Enrique Iglesias's 'Bailamos'.

Let's ***take off*** and get this show on the road.

This song ***takes you*** *back* to the 90s. It's a song most of us *grew up* with.

Sean Paul celebrates his 40th birthday today. Happy Birthday, Sean! Let's ***drink to*** this awesome dude's health.

All evidence indicates (***points to*** the fact) that things will ***settle down*** soon in Syria.

Use of Language Debriefing

Debriefing is an evaluation process that takes place at the end of each day or the record of each segment or on a regular basis. The frequency of the meeting depends on the urgency with which the discussion must occur or the evaluation must take place. In the context of radio station, a debriefing meeting must occur at least once a day.

Debriefing is an opportunity for the members of the team to come together and discuss the highlights of the day. The editor gets an opportunity to briefly run through the events, congratulate all those who worked well and successfully completed their parts and to point out the mistakes and pull up those whose work needs improvement. It is an opportunity to analyse and make a study of all the factors that contributed to the success of a particular programme, determine ways in which the same level of success can be emulated for the next edition of the same programme or achieved in another format and to examine and find areas that demand improvement.

The language that is used in debriefing is not very formal though it is not extremely informal either. It follows the normal patterns and structures of the formal, though it is usually sans the longwinded openings associated with formal meetings (or salutations, if it is written) and exceptionally formal language. The language must convey matter-of-factness and contribute to conciseness. It is authoritative and offers constructive criticism in an objective manner.

Commissioning brief

It is a document that is furnished by the station and details the general facts about a specific programme. It is a reference point for producers/ makers who wish to create programmes for individual broadcasters. For instance, the BBC commissions many of its programmes on Radio4 and has detailed **commissioning briefs** that outline its expectations and specifications.

Briefs provide guidelines and information on what is expected from the producers or creators. A **commissioning brief** clearly indicates the timeslot of the programme, programme type (genre – drama, comedy, special events, etc.), duration, transmission period, editorial guidelines to be followed while writing the synopsis, price that will be paid, audience (age group, social group, gender, etc.) and the eligibility criteria for the creative makers/producers.

Vocabulary in commissioning briefs

Slot: It refers to the time (day/night, afternoon/evening/night) during which a programme is brought out. Each slot caters to different audience, though audience could overlap.

Duration: It is the length of a programme (normally 22 minutes for a feature, soap etc). It may also be referred to as running time.

Producer: The head of the show who arranges finance and coordinates the production. In Indian parlance it would refer to the financer.

Audience: The target group or the consumer of the radio show. Audience is categorized on the basis of age, gender, socio-economic status, occupation or demographics.

Genre: This refers to the nature/content of the programme. It could be comedy, drama, romance etc.

Transmission period: The expected date/month of transmission. As most programmes are commissioned and produced well in advance, it is important for the producers to know the time gap to transmission.

Eligibility: Refers to the qualification/track record of the producer. While educational qualification is not the ultimate criteria, previous experience normally stand one in good stead.

Price: The amount that will be paid by the station to the producer as payment for services (for production of the programme).

Radio Presenter

The radio presenter becomes the unseen face and the heard voice of the radio station. It is his/her personality that decides the image of the radio station. It is also the radio presenter who sets the style and tone of the station and presents news, views, information and even chatter in a manner that is at once engaging and entertaining. He/she provides lead-in to programmes, conducts interviews, presents facts and news, interacts with callers during phone-ins and is generally the person that the audience associates with the station.

Being a radio presenter thus demands that one does a variety of roles. It is important to have a deep understanding about the topic on hand. You have to be objective and take a bird's eye view of the news and also ask the right questions which will provide answers that lead to the heart of the matter. A presenter is jack of all trades who is politically and socially aware, keeps abreast with current events, has knowledge of music and arts, a researcher who is concerned with feedback and audience preferences and a team player as radio production is not solitary endeavour. Therefore, he or she must be:

- able to analyse information with an incisive and questioning attitude;
- able to draw the threads of various agreements and viewpoints together to present a summary or draw conclusions;
- an entertainer who can charm the audience;
- aware that you are constantly being heard and graded and
- be careful about the content and the language that is used.

Writing for Radio Programmes

The radio offers a variety of programmes. The purpose of each programme varies. Some are meant to inform and educate, others fulfil the ultimate purpose of entertaining. With changes in programme format and target audience, come changes in the style and form of language used. While words that convey briskness and immediacy is used when writing a news script, an informal, chatty or everyday conversational language is used in a phone-in programme. A discussion uses semi-formal language. A radio play relies heavily on the voice of actors and sound effects to communicate the theme while an illustrative talk calls for a different approach.

The voice(s) used is important as the text has to be conveyed clearly and audibly. The writer relies on words, music and sound effect to create images in the minds of the listeners. Research, flair for writing and imagination are pre-requisites for scripting any radio programme. The script must convey the nuances of the situation, overcoming a lack of visuals and relying on sound alone. That is the challenge that the writer must face and surmount.

Interviews

Interviews are a kind of feature and are an extremely popular form on the radio. It can form a programme on its own (that is a feature) or may be used during news to supplement or add extra information. The interviewee can state his/her opinion and add information on the topic that is being discussed. An interview must be used during a news story only if it can add something extra, something that is new or hitherto unheard of or looks at a different facet of the story. An interview adds credibility to the news as the opinion may be provided by an expert or leading and trustworthy figure. It is also evident that the opinion that is being stated is not professed by the station but is being put forward by an individual.

Radio interviews can take different forms. It may be in the following forms:

Studio interviews are the ones that are recorded in the studio. As there is no 'noise', the quality of these interviews is excellent. This is a deliberated form and hence is structured and controlled. It is also well researched and the final result is a product that is carefully thought out and executed.

Spot interviews are used normally during the course of delivery of news, in features, especially biographical or opinion pieces, in documentaries, etc. They are generally short and its length is determined by the amount of information that can be conveyed without taxing the listener's receptive and grasping capacities. Spot interviews either provide a point of view or additional information.

Field interviews: Interviews conducted outside the studio are termed as ***Field interviews.*** They provide onsite information to the audience and serve the purpose of taking them to the place of action and making the event/news come alive for them. Such interviews can vary in length.

Vocabulary used in interviews

1. Q&A (Question and Answer) or two-way: Interviews used in radio news reports. The reporter or the interviewee is asked questions by the presenter or news reader.
2. **Vox Pop (from VoxPopuli)**: This invites comments or opinions from the public or the man on the street on the issue or topic that is of interest to the public and under discussion.

Pointers

While preparing for the interview points that should be kept in mind are:

- There is no substitute for research. In order to plan a good interview, ask insightful questions or cover all aspects of an issue (with special attention paid to controversial aspects). The right candidate can be identified through research.

- What is the focus of the interview?
- The interview should be audience-centric. The interviewer should be able to elicit answers to all the questions that arise in the minds of the listeners. That is to say he/she should be able to anticipate their questions and satisfy their curiosity by providing them with answers.
- Key areas of interest or areas that will be covered must be decided beforehand.

Pre-interview

- Record the interview in a quiet location so that the sound quality is not affected.
- Check voice levels and equipment.

During the interview

- Wear headphones while recording. Check the quality as the recording progresses.
- Microphones should be carefully positioned. Modern microphones are sensitive and should be used with care.
- Always record more than you need. Ask more questions than you need to. This leaves you room to manoeuvre and structure the interview in ways that are different from what you initially envisioned.
- Where possible, allow the interviewee to introduce himself/herself. Let them provide their names, designation and other details. This will help familiarize the audience with the sound of the speaker.
- Interviewer talk time should be less. Ensure that the questions are short and open ended which provides scope for the subject to talk.
- Ensure that the interviewee is at ease.
- Questions must be asked in a logical sequence.

- A good interviewer is a good listener and is able to dig in and ask questions based on the information provided by the interviewee.

Excerpt of Radio Interview (Script):
Sample Radio Interview
This is a script of the interview between Fearne Cotton and Leona Lewis for BBC Radio one's Live Lounge

0–3 secs	**Show jingle:** This is radio one's Live Lounge hour
	SFX: Music bed
4–6 secs	**Fearne:** Now it's time to cross over live to Maida Vale live to say hello to Leona Lewis
6–8 secs	**Leona:** Hello
8–10 secs	**Fearne:** How are you?
10–12 secs	**Leona:** I'm good than you
12–18 secs	**Fearne:** It's lovely to have you in the Live Lounge, very excited about this and loads of people on the text cannot wait to hear you sing
18–20 secs	**Leona:** Oh thank you
20–25 secs	**Fearne:** You must have some nice fond memories of the Live Lounge because it's obviously the first time that you performed Run live in the Live Lounge
25–30 secs	**SFX:** Archive clip of Leona singing Run in the Live Lounge
30–35 secs	**Leona:** Yeah it was and it was cool getting it all together and working with a bank and you know its such a great studio so it was really good.

Source: BBC Radio 1

Radio News

News is a staple on radio and listeners rely on radio to keep them updated. The radio is capable of transmitting breaking news and takes the listener to the place of action. This feature gives it a distinct advantage over the print medium. The fact that it is mobile and portable and can be accessed anywhere within a station's transmission limits gives it an edge over the cumbersome television. Modern technology ensures that radio can be accessed on mobile phones thereby making it even more accessible, and satellite radio has efficiently overcome the earlier disadvantage of transmission boundaries of the radio stations. One can access stations from across the globe via satellite radio.

Defining news

- The events/occurrences that make their way into the news bulletin are determined by what is termed as news value. If it has value – that is if it is likely to appeal to a large section of the audience – then it is selected and included in the bulletin. Whether it is radio, TV or print media, the values remain the same.
- Factors that determine value include Time lines, Impact, Proximity, Significance, Conflict, Confrontation and Prominence which are discussed in detail in the first module. The Human Interest – any event that has the potential to touch hearts, elicit laughter, inspire or stir up emotions, has also got value.

Scripting radio news

As mentioned previously, the script follows the two-column format. While scripting there are certain golden rules to be followed to make it effective. The writer has to remember that the news is being written for the ear and hence must be as clear and concise as possible. To do so:

- Use a combination of short sentences, simple language and easily recognizable words.
- Adopt a conversational tone without resorting to colloquialism.
- Avoid clichés.
- Make the copy as lean as possible; have short paragraphs. But cover all aspects of the story (Who, What, Where, When, Why).
- Write with flair but ethically and responsibly. Be objective and correct.

- Use direct quotes with caution. Avoid it as far as possible unless relevant as it is difficult to distinguish the quote from the rest of the copy. As far as possible use bites/actualities of well-known people, as these voices are familiar. When using direct quotes prepare the listener well in advance so that they know whose opinion (and in which context) is being stated and voice they may expect.
- When using acronyms, care must be taken. In case the acronym is pronounced in much the same way that words are (e.g., NASA), then it should be typed out in caps. But in the case of acronyms like ISRO where individual letters are sounded out, use the following format: I-S-R-O.
- Approximate numbers. It is better to say *Approximately or nearly 300* rather than 287.
- Write out numbers One through Ten. Use numerals, in case of numbers greater than ten.
- Include plenty of sound bites and interviews so that the script does not make use of the news reader's voice alone.

Form

Each individual piece of news/each story is written following the structure: Lead – Pars/Supporting paragraphs – Conclusion/Closing statements.

Lead: It is the first paragraph or the opening statement of the story. It informs the listener what the story is going to be about and serves to hook the listener. It will throw light on the most important aspect(s) of the story and provide clues as to how the story would develop. A short lead works best.

Pars: This follows the lead and forms the second and third sentences. It is an extension of the lead in the sense that it provides facts and explains the lead.

Conclusion: This reinforces the message that has been given out in the lead and the subsequent statements. It forms the final paragraph or 'par'. It summarizes or re-tells the story in brief.

News Bulletins

A news bulletin must contain a mix of stories and be 'balanced'. It must include national, international, local, entertainment and sports news so that listeners feel that they have received a 'complete' range of news.

The news that is selected depends on the policies and philosophy of individual radio stations. The order in which the news is presented is decided on the basis of its newsworthiness. As you may have assumed, the kind of audience who tune into the station, whether the news will affect them, impact, proximity and timeliness – these elements determine the selection.

*The **lead story*** is often the event or news that just happened and that impacts the audience the most. Related stories are presented together. For instance, cricket and tennis news will be grouped together, while international events or financial news will be presented together. This allows the announcer to move smoothly from related stories, without jumping back and forth and enabling a natural progression in the presentation of various stories.

It may be noted that the morning news bulletin often contains many international and national stories of events that happened overnight, whereas the afternoon bulletin is normally focussed on local or regional news. News stories get pushed down the bulletin as the hours pass, until they are fully replaced by newer events.

As Radio is a 'now' medium, broadcasters are constantly on the look out to 'scoop' competitors and to be the first to 'break' the news. Care must be taken to check and confirm facts before going on air, even while racing to be the winner in the ratings race.

Exercise: Identify errors and make corrections in the radio news copy

1. Police searching for bodies at a former children's home on Jersey say 166 people have now come forward with claims of abuse. 40 potential suspects identified.
2. The House of Commons experienced a major security breach when environmental campaigners climbed onto the roof of the House of Commons.

3. As part of its new drug strategy, the Government plans to cut welfare hand-outs to addicts. Conservatives describe this move as gimmick.
4. "Cabinet minutes should not be released under the Freedom of Information Act," says a former Chair of the Joint Intelligence Committee.
5. Damage from previous night's earthquake will likely cost more than ten million pounds to repair, insurers say.

Radio Talk Show

A talk show can take different forms. Depending on the format that suits the station, it could be a show hosted by a radio personality that touches upon a variety of topics, a one-on-one interview (an interaction between the host and a guest or two/reporter) or a radio discussion where a topic is debated and opinions of several people are sought.

The central figure in programmes of this sort is the host or interviewer who also acts as a moderator in the case of radio discussions. S/He has the task of initiating the *tete-a-tete* or discussion, driving it forward and directing its course by asking relevant and interesting questions. S/He is responsible for the selection of topics and people to be interviewed, in determining the format that the show will take and finalizing the sound bites that will be included. To a large extent, it is the quality of the host that makes a good talk show. If s/he has the ability to draw people out, create a friendly ambience and adopt an approach that is unique to her/him, the ultimate result would be a show that is different from the rest. The personality of the host determines the personality of the show. The choice of the invitee(s) or the persons who have been selected to take part in the discussion is important. Efforts must be taken to ensure that the show is a platform to express a plethora of opinions and viewpoints, so that the talk/discussion can be considered complete in the sense that all views are represented.

Talk shows open with a salutation and signature music. It is peppered with conversational phrases and filler sounds that give the talk a sense of ease and everyday variety to it. This makes the show interactive and draws the listeners in. Sly asides, humorous remarks and contemporary anecdotes are common features. ***Voice, intonation and stress*** are also important elements that determine the popularity of a talk show.

See below an excerpt from the popular talk show *Jeremy Vine Show* on BBC Radio 2. Note the features mentioned above in the following copy.

JEREMY: Welcome to the Jeremy Vine Show on BBC Radio 2.

MUSIC

Here we are! Today, Are you fed up with automatic telephone menus. Someone has invented a way around them. You tell us your system. The Oklahoma tornado claims more than 90 lives. Have you experienced a twister? Plus, US 'swivel-eyed loon' and proud of it. We ask Nigel Farage if it is possible to take that insulting phrase as a compliment. And Maurice Saatchi says it wasn't just the cancer that killed his wife. It was the treatment she had.

SIGNATURE MUSIC

We have at least 17 ways to get in touch. There's Facebook, there's Twitter, if you look me up there. There's email vine@bbc.co.uk. And there's the phone number 0500 288 291. Only problem with the phone is, I have to point out, the calls are free from most landlines but some networks and mobile operators will charge you. I think we know that by now. Let's go to the news on First and see what's breaking with the very latest…

REPORTER: Thank you, Jeremy. Rescue workers are continuing to search for bodies in the rubble of buildings devastated by huge tornado in the suburbs of the American city of Oklahoma. At least 91 people are thought to have died, including 20 children after their school took a direct hit from the storm. A Christian Minister in the Oklahoma city Pastor Ben Glava said the community was in shock. (SOUND BITE of Pastor)

Radio Reviews

Reviews are a kind of feature and are extremely popular. As they provide facts, information and opinion about a variety of events/things such as movies, art exhibitions, music, books, etc, they guide and help listeners form an opinion about the event/programme being discussed and reach a decision about whether to view/read or not.

A review should be objective and fair and should not be vindictive or petty. When offering a negative opinion, the reviewer must state reasons why he has reached the said opinion. A balanced review means that both the positives and negatives are discussed.

A review should also adopt a holistic approach. In the case of a film review, aspects such as acting, direction, cinematography, music, art, etc. must be commented upon. The review must be placed within a context and the reviewer may compare/contrast the story/direction/acting with other works in the same genre or previous films by the same director/actor. The same techniques may also be used in the case of music reviews and book reviews, though the points of focus would differ. In the case of a music review, the relative merits of the piece of music, the rendering, emotional overtones, etc. would be discussed. It must also make a note of the quality of the piece in comparison to music of a similar kind (genre).

Reviews normally include clips of the music so that the listener can hear and get a better understanding of what the reviewer is trying to state. Is it a happy/sad/peppy/youthful song? Does it convey emotions with ease? This is also one line of enquiry that the reviewer must follow.

It is also a normal practice to rate a creative piece. Each reviewer can develop his/her own unique/individual rating scale, e.g., 3.5, 3 and ½, 3 and a half stars, etc.

The reviewer must be an expert or someone who is well versed and knowledgeable in the field. His/her opinions must be based on facts, not mere opinions, likes or dislikes. S/He must develop a signature style, which will set the reviewer apart from others.

The language used in a review must be simple and graphic (descriptive). The active form of speech is used and the words must convey energy. The review must be in the form of a dialogue with the listener as the silent partner. It must be conversational.

Music Programmes

Music itself may be used in the following ways on radio:

- To entertain;
- To identify it with a certain programme (jingles or signature music), create individuality and
- As a production device in the form of background scores etc.

Music programmes have a format that is extremely popular with both the audience and broadcasters. Songs are used as *'fillers'* to *provide breaks* between programmes and to break the monotony of listening to the anchor. It is a welcome break after a heavier format such as a discussion, news bulletin, interview, etc.

Stations often have pure music programmes or music features with half-hour slots set apart for playing songs at regular intervals. These sorts of programmes normally have an announcer or radio jockey (RJ) who introduces each song briefly. Example of music feature could be a programme like *Top Twenty Countdown, VOA Music Mix, BBC's* Alan Simpson, *Top 40,* etc. Radio spots dedicated to music of a particular decade (e.g., 1980s or 1990s western music) create moods and inspire nostalgia.

Radio often has phone-in programmes where the caller can call up, speak to the RJ and request a song from a wide selection. Callers can dedicate songs as well. The kind of programme where callers pick songs from a given selection is called a Jukebox.

Another kind of programme that is related to music or inspired is a quiz or Question-and-Answer programme. The DJ plays a part of the song and asks the caller questions based on it. After the Q&A session, the song may be played in part or in its entirety.

Broadcasters are conscious of the crowd that they are targeting and their demographics. They often conduct surveys so that they are able to read audience demand for different kinds of music. A play list is compiled according to these demands.

Special programmes or features may be aired dedicated to certain singers, bands, music directors or genres.

Some songs may be inappropriate for broadcast because of the lyrics. The station has to make sure that it is not breaking broadcasting policies when playing music.

Phone-in

This is a popular format and allows for interactivity. This programming allows the distant and sometimes disconnected media to move from the impersonal to the personal, thus bridging the gap between the station and the listeners. The RJ plays a significant role in success of this programme. The personality of the programme is determined by the RJ. Though the basic format of the programme remains the same, each station tries to bring in some level of innovation in its presentation. It is a combination of the style of presentation, the personality of the RJ and the quality of the programme that determine its popularity.

The phone-in programme is an informal programme. The RJ must possess the gift of the gab, be genuinely interested in people, charming and have a talent for starting, maintaining and entertaining conversations with callers, drawing them in and engaging them. S/He must also possess knowledge of the topic – music, film, etc. S/He must take care not to use offensive terms or language. These are programmes that serve as a platform for creative criticism on contemporary social issues.

Radio Plays

The radio is known for its innovative programmes and for bringing out new programmes in new formats. While there is no dearth of creative features/other programmes in the radio, works that have attained immense popularity in other formats are usually translated/transformed into radio features. It is not unusual to hear a book being narrated or a drama/play being performed on radio. *Akashvani* Malayalam channels continue with the practice of transmitting sound tracks of Malayalam movies over the radio. One can listen to the sounds and 'see' the movie in the mind's eye. Despite this being about the crudest form of translation and while entertaining, it is not a challenging form to create/produce. Similarly, books, plays and poems may be read out. The importance of voice cannot be ignored in the case of such readings.

It is challenging to take a book/play and create a mutated form that is tailor-made to play to those characteristics of the radio that set it apart from others, and suit the medium itself. Some parts/aspects are highlighted, while others are ignored all together because the same cannot be successfully translated into the target medium.

There are certain narratives that would be impossible to communicate over the radio. Stories set in imaginary worlds, horror and fantasy or stories on supernatural beings like faeries, valkyries, shape shifters, etc. cannot be conveyed effectively. Thrillers would suffer the same fate. The creator/producer of such a work would have to find innovative ways to express such storylines.

When translating/transforming a play for the radio, the writer must be aware of the pitfalls. S/He must decide at the outset what elements can be incorporated and transferred effectively and what would have to be left out. S/He must ask her/himself whether such omissions would seriously undermine the thread, scope and direction of the story. When adapting a story from one medium to another, an important consideration is the issue of copyright. The station must not only buy the copyright or the right to use the source material, it must also gain permission to make those changes that may be necessary to tailor the material to suit radio.

Exercises

1. Write a script for a radio feature on the following topics:
   a. Nawab Mansoor Ali Khan Pataudi
   b. Cult status of cricketers
2. Prepare a list of 20 questions for an interview with Lionel Messi.
3. Write a script for a radio profile with a political leader highlighting his/her political career, stance, challenges faced, issues he/she has lobbied, personal life, etc.
4. Write a script for a radio discussion on the following:
   a. Cricket and the Underworld – a troubling nexus?

5. Create a radio play based on any one of Uroob's (P.C. Kuttikrishnan) works. Write the script keeping in mind that the literary work is being translated for an aural medium.
6. Create a radio advertisement for one of the following:
   a. Soap
   b. Umbrella
   c. Bottled water
7. Compare the style and form of a radio phone-in music programme that broadcasts songs from 1950s – 2000 to a similar programme that features current and newer songs. Do you see any differences and similarities? Note the same. Now create a 30-minutes phone-in music programme (complete with RJ's dialogues, songs, advertisements, etc.) focussing either on new songs or old ones.
8. Write a script for a radio documentary. Choose a social or political issue as your theme.
9. Select a social issue or question for public debate. Create a Radio VoxPopuli and gather different opinions and viewpoints on the same. The final piece must be complete with narration.
10. Create a radio news bulletin. Duration: 10 minutes. Topics should cover National, International, Regional, Economy, Sports stories, etc.
11. Write a script for a morning show on radio.
12. Develop an idea for a programme in the graveyard slot.

CHAPTER 3

Visual Media

Introduction

Television (TV) is one of the most influential media today. The advantage that this medium enjoys over the traditional media like newspaper and radio is that it is audio-visual. It makes it possible to see and hear about events happening in far off places, even while one remains within the four walls of one's home. This ability of TV to enter homes, and thus lives, makes it a personal medium.

It is a powerful medium that has the power to influence and affect human lives.

Creating TV Programmes

Television brings to its viewers a variety of programmes ranging from news bulletins, serials or soaps, music- and film-based programmes to features like interviews, live shows, sports-based programmes, etc.

The primary step in the creation of a piece for TV is to come up with a concept or idea for a programme. Finding a TV channel to broadcast, writing the script, finding the right cast and crew, the shooting itself, editing – these are the activities that follow. The programme production process may be divided into three stages – preproduction, production and postproduction. The preparations before the actual shooting fall into the preproduction stage; the shooting of the programme is termed as production and activities such as editing, sound mixing that follows the production process are termed as postproduction events.

Preproduction

This is one of the most important stages as it is during this stage that the story idea evolves and the creators or producers plan for the execution of the project. Preproduction involves everything from scriptwriting and writing the screenplay to the identifying and contracting the services of cast and crew, booking studio, determining shooting schedule, hiring equipments and studios, identifying locations for outdoor shoots, raising finance, etc.

The preproduction phase prepares the team for the actual shooting of the programme. In the case of serials, unlike in the case of a single-episode programme or miniseries, the production does not follow the straight forward preproduction-production-postproduction sequence. Rather it follows a cyclic pattern moving from the preproduction to the final stage and then back again to preproduction for the next set in the series. Preproduction cannot be completed at one go, as the story is constantly evolving and changing.

Television Scripts

Format

A two-column script is used for television as well. This script is used for all kinds of TV programmes, including news. In a TV script, the right-hand column is called Video and the left–hand column is titled Audio. The spoken words/copy, sound effects and music are detailed in the Audio column. Everything that you would see on the TV screen (the visuals) along with the nature of the visuals (nature of shot, use of graphics, time taken and other pertinent facts) and general production information – camera angles, action, scenery and stage directions is included in the left-hand Video column.

There are three types of scripts for a play or drama:

- The page is divided into two. The Video column contains everything that people will see on the screen – action, people, places, etc. The Audio column is for everything that is heard, which includes dialogue, music or any other sounds.
- The script is written only on the right–hand side of the page. The blank space on the left is used for instructions, descriptions and notes. All dialogues are written or typed in small letters; all instructions or descriptions are in caps.
- Final shooting script, which contains detailed directions for the director, cameramen and technicians, serves as a blueprint for shooting.
- It is put together by many people who have a visual concept of what the product should look like – writer, director, cameramen, producer, etc. The dialogues and the camera instructions may be numbered.

Scripting

The basis of any script is the story idea or theme of the programme. The story is then developed till it assumes a final shape and form.

Research plays an important role in developing the script. The audience is a priority when developing a script, as this factor determines the manner in which the script develops, the setting, the cultural and linguistic context of the story and the manner of delivery.

Once the programme idea has been thrashed out, the treatment must be decided. The scriptwriter must make a call and determine which approach works best – romance, drama, humour, action, adventure or any other.

The scriptwriter is constantly pressed to come up with new ideas and new ways of expressing age-old tales. For instance, the storyline of any crime or detective series would involve crimes being committed and the attempts made by law or private detectives to apprehend the criminals and solve the case. The essential formula remains the same. Thus, we may conclude that it is the characterization, setting, manner of presentation, dialogues, etc. that make each programme unique, entertaining and a hit with the audience.

The next step is the writing of a synopsis. A synopsis is a brief summary of the programme idea and story. This helps the writer and others involved in the project to develop focus; it sets limits or perimeters and to communicate the essence of the programme in a brief manner.

The draft script, which helps the writer determine how to go about telling the story using dialogues, sounds and visuals, is then developed. The writer must remember that he is writing for an audio-visual medium and the script is a blueprint for what will be seen on the screen. **The shots, angles, props, music, other sounds** all play an important role in '**narrating**' the story. From the draft script, the storyboard is developed and this translates the script into visual and gives the production team an idea of what the scene looks like. Detailed shooting instructions may be included. It is a useful tool as it helps the team identify those elements that do not work and to fine-tune the project. A shooting script is a more detailed version of the storyboard and is a device that is useful to the director, cameraman and technicians.

Script writing

Writing is a creative process and involves the ability to tell a tale. The story has to be presented in an interesting and entertaining manner. Depending on the programme format, the techniques of writing change. But there are certain common rules that may be adopted when writing a script. They are:

- Use a style that is easy and conversational;
- Use simple language;
- Use active voice;
- Use verbs, as it denotes action;
- Use adjectives (except in news stories);
- Use an engaging and personal tone;

- Use direct approach;
- Use techniques that will generate interest;
- Must convey the message clearly;
- Must be conceived in such as manner that explores different facets of an issue and
- Write for the audience. Ask yourself what questions the audience wants answered or what they want from the programme.

In the case of a news report, scripting happens after news stories have been selected for a certain bulletin.

Use of Formal and Informal/Conversational Language

The language used in TV veers from the formal to the informal and casual depending the programme and context in which it is used. TV news, for instance, demands matter-of-fact and formal language. The purpose of the language here is to give an impression of authority, (and thus credibility; tone plays an important role in this) and to communicate as much as can be conveyed using minimum number of words. The interactive session during the news merits a slightly different approach and the tone adopted is different from the one used in news. It could be in the form of a package (includes interview with the reporter or a phone/studio interview with someone who has information/opinion that add to the story). Here, the attempt is to elicit answers. So the sentences are framed as questions. This is one area where question tags are used. For instance,

Sentence 1: *You have contributed substantially to the project, haven't you? Can you elaborate?*

The same idea can also be communicated in the following manner:

Sentence 2: *You have contributed substantially to the project. Can you comment?*

In the case of the first sentence, the first part with the question tag by and in itself invites a response; the '*Can you comment?*' merely emphasizes one's desire to hear more (a desire already implied in the first part). The tone is important as the shades of meaning change completely with a change in tone. In radio and television, language alone does not decide the impact of the message; the tone is equally important. It may also be noted that the '*Can you comment?*' makes it more conversational.

A discussion depends on the participants and in this case the language used may be a mixture of formal and conversational depending on the participants, their socio-cultural backgrounds and, most particularly, the topic under discussion.

Use of Collocations

Collocations are combinations of words that imply a certain meaning and are used by native speakers of English. Collocations help in the naturalization of speech.

Examples of collocations that are frequently heard in the media would include *rich and famous, weapons of mass destruction, break the rule or break the law, make a difference, pay respect, pay someone a visit, go to war, come under attack, go out of business, come to an agreement, annual turnover, break off negotiations, close a deal, go bankrupt, go into partnership, make a profit (or loss), popular/national media,* etc.

Some examples

The US accuses North Korea of developing *weapons of mass destruction.*

North Korea *goes to war* with South Korea.

Mahindra *closes deal* with Renault.

Exercise: Use collocations in five sentences of your own. Ensure that the style and vocabulary suit TV.

Modal verbs

Modal verbs are verbs that are used in a very irregular/different manner in English. Its usage is a challenge for non-natives. Yet in the course of speaking/writing English, it must be used. Modal verbs include ***Can, Could, May, Might, Must, Will, Would, Shall, Should and Ought to.***

Examples:
May I direct your attention to the issue of rising prices? (Permission, polite)

What can you tell us about the steps that the government ***would*** adopt to counter this? (Proposal)

Could you enlighten us on the topic of drug cartels in the US? (Willingness)

You ***must*** watch this movie. (Obligation)

The claims just ***can't*** be true. (Probability)

He ***can*** speak five Indian languages and four foreign languages. (Ability

Exercise: Use modal verbs to communicate information

1. ______ you tell us with absolute certainty that none have been trapped in the burning building?
2. Experts opine that the mining authority ______ drill a separate tunnel to get to the trapped miners.
3. You ______ watch this movie.
4. He ______ quit the game on this high note.
5. The PM has yet to arrive. He ______ running late

Television News

Television has changed the way we receive, process and respond to news. Television is a 'now' medium and is able to cater to people's desire to know things immediately and watch events unfold. It has immediate impact, the kind that can only be matched by the web. Even Radio cannot compete with TV as it is a blind medium.

News on television may be presented in three forms. It can be a reporter-narrated story. This story may be reported from the scene of action/outdoors, in response to the anchor's queries. The first one is preferable as it adds credibility and it is able to involve the audience in the process of narration. The anchor or newsreader and the audience await the reporter's response together. In another format, the news may be reported by the newsreader as a voice-over, with graphics or video being shown. Briefs are another form of news. This technique is used for news events that do not have high news value or visuals. Here, the news may be read out by the newsreader; only minimum details are provided.

News value

Every piece of news will not find its way into a news bulletin. Time is a valuable commodity in TV and only the most important news is presented. Selection of right news is determined by its news value, which is a combination of many factors as has been mentioned in module I. Apart from this, as TV is a visual medium, the selected news must be visually appealing. News events that appeal visually and impact the senses are selected.

Writing TV news

Television news demands a distinct style of writing. It is often called headline service. TV news usually, unless the story demands time, provides a headline or introduction to the news, followed by only the most important supporting facts.

TV news copy must be short and punchy. The writer must remember that the news on TV is heard, not read. So the shorter the news is, the better it is. The normal time limit that is set aside for a news story is 20–40 seconds and the average number of words used in a sentence is between 13 and 14. Clarity is very important. There is no scope for a playback and so the news must be understood the first and only time it is heard and seen. The story must be progressed logically and be well structured. This contributes to comprehensibility. ***So the emphasis is***

on the 'What' and the 'Where' rather than on 'Why' or 'How'. The words should be complementary to the visuals being shown. It must attract the attention of the viewer and hold it. It must communicate the story to the audience.

Other factors should be kept in mind when writing for TV:

- The language must be simple and conversational. It must avoid difficult to pronounce words, foreign words and phrases, usage of 'former' and 'latter' (difficult to distinguish), etc.
- Names must be repeated and use of pronouns should be avoided.
- Figures and statistics must be dealt with caution.
- Unnecessary words must be avoided.
- Adjectives and adverbs have no place in a news copy.
- A conversational style must be adopted.
- Use everyday words and language.
- Adopt grammatically sound and simple style. Avoid colloquialism and slang.
- The news copy must convey a sense of urgency. This can be achieved by making use of the present tense and active voice. This will help convey immediacy.
- Words like 'now', 'this morning', 'today', 'a few minutes ago' convey a sense of immediacy and makes the news sound fresh. Use the present perfect tense if the past tense is unavoidable

The lead is an important part of the TV news copy. It acts as a hook to catch the interest of the viewer and to briefly introduce the story. It sets the stage for the story. It must not give away all the details. Each story must also be wrapped up, so that viewers are aware when one ends and the next begins. A wrap-up summarizes and provides a satisfactory end to the story.

While writing the broadcast copy the writer has to keep a few rules in mind. They are:

- Tough-to-pronounce and unfamiliar names must be written out phonetically.
- Abbreviations must be avoided.
- Names of organizations, places, days of the week, etc. must be written out fully.

- The only exception to this rule is when the abbreviation or acronym is more familiar sounding that the name itself, e.g., AIDS.
- Titles should precede names, e.g., *'The Indian President Pranab Mukherjee announced ...'* rather than *'Pranab Mukherjee, the Indian President, today stated...'*.
- Symbols like E.g. %, &, # should not be used on copy.
- For numerals write out the numbers from 'one' to 'nine' and 'eleven' as well. The numeral '11' can be easily mistaken. Figures or numerals may be used for the number '10' and for numbers from '12' to '999'.
- Spell out words such as thousand, lakh, million, billion, etc. Make statistics easily comprehensible. For example, the number 76,00,000 can be written as 7.6 million.
- Use as little punctuation as possible. Commas are the exception as they tell the newsreader where to pause and give him/her a better idea of how the report should be read.
- Use few quotes as part of the script. It is difficult to communicate the fact that what is being read out by the newsreader is a quote as opposed to copy written by the station.
- Clear attribution is difficult to achieve. If a quote is being used, show a graphic carrying the same and name of the source.
- Corrections should be clear. If a word is to be edited or substituted, it must be clearly crossed and the new word should be clearly written.

EXAMPLE: TV news script

VIDEO	**AUDIO**
NEWSREADER O/C	Good Evening and welcome to the news at 7. The Headlines.
GRAPHICS	BJP demands PM's resignation over Coal Allocation Scam.
VO	Indo-Pak border tensions escalate.
TRT – 6 SECONDS	

Exercise

Develop a script for a news bulletin from the news given below. Prioritize the news according to news value.

- Fifth bird flu death as China sounds high alert.
- Italian PM dials Salman Khurshid as NIA books marines for murder.
- Maoists attack rail tracks, buildings in Jharkhand
- NATO strike kills 10 Afghan children. Provokes great anger in the war-torn country.
- Stosur, Wozniacki cruise; Venus struggles in WTA Tour's Family Circle Cup.
- Margaret Thatcher dead at 87.

Soaps

In popular parlance serials or TV series are called soaps. The name 'soap' comes from the fact these programmes were initially sponsored by soap manufacturing companies. A series or serial has a basic premise or a storyline. The plot unfolds as the series progresses and the final episode of the series brings the story and subplots to conclusion and wraps up loose ends. Each episode could deal with a new event/issue/crisis (*Criminal Minds, White Collar, CSI, Bones, Arjun)* or it may continue from where it ended in the previous episode and seek a resolution (most Hindi and regional serials work on this premise). The plot of a series is riddled with crisis. It is the conflict and resolution of the conflict that drives the story forward. Most of the main characters are featured in every episode. Recurring supporting characters is another feature.

Characterization is a vital element and the characters in a series are much better developed than a character in a film. The relationship between a character in a film and the viewer lasts a couple of hours at the most but the relationship with TV characters is more organic. The story may also progress by revealing more facets of a character's personality; tracing their growth or evolution and sharing snippets that provide clues as to why they behave in a certain way.

A good series is extremely engaging, pulls the audience to it everyday (or however frequently it is telecast), creates a rapport with its audience by showcasing events or situations that the audience can enjoy (*Big Bang Theory)* or understand or which fulfils their fantasy or their taste for the fantastic (*True Blood, Game of Thrones*).

A series is meant for a particular target audience and hence the language and references – social and cultural – are ones that the audience must be able to understand and relate to (however, distantly). Along with the visuals, it is the dialogues that propels the story forward and entertains the audience. The language that is used follows the simple and conversational style and must suit the characters. For instance, a college-going yuppie converses in a style that is vastly different from a banker or a curator. The language used by each character must reflect his/her background and subtly refer to his/her age, gender, education, social, economic and cultural standing.

Examples

(From *Big Bang Theory*)

Sheldon: *I can't believe he fired me.*

Leonard: *Well, you did call him a "glorified high school science teacher whose last successful experiment was lighting his own farts."*

Sheldon: *In my defense, I prefaced that with, "with all due respect."*

(Sheldon's dialogues veer to the formal; the reference to his previous comments indicate disdain and irreverence; Leonard's dialogues are conversational and humorous)

Howard: *(to Mary, Sheldon's mother) Forgive me for being so bold, but I now see where Sheldon gets his charming good looks.* (Formal)

Mary: *Honey, that ain't gonna work, but you keep trying.* (Informal, colloquial)

(From *White Collar*)

Mozzie (quoting St. Augustine): *Love is a temporary madness. It erupts like an earthquake and then subsides.* (Descriptive)

Peter: *We woke a giant, Neal.*

Neal: *You ready to take down a giant.*

Peter: *Don't forget your sling shot.*

(Biblical reference to David and the Goliath; descriptive; punchy)

Avery: *If we do business off the books, we should talk off the clocks.*

(Use of idioms; colloquial; sharp)

Interviews and Talk Shows

TV Interviews can assume many forms. One form is a feature which aims at exploring the lives of well-known individuals by asking questions that elicits opinions and responses on a variety of topics. The focus of such interviews reveal as much as possible about the subject (who is famous, popular and a celebrity) by asking well-thought-out questions. These are normally called talk shows. They satisfy the viewer's curiosity to know more about the subject and are a popular staple in TV programming.

The other form of interviews is even more common and they are normally incorporated into or form a part of another programme like news story, chat show, documentary, profiles, etc. These are statements of opinions and reveal the perspective of an individual with regard to an issue. They add credibility to the programme and allow attribution. ***Straight out of the horse's mouth*** is a phrase that is applicable in this context. They are also a means of presenting a plethora of opinions together on the same platform and satisfy the demand to represent all points of view in a straightforward and efficient manner. They also help to break the monotony of the programme and add life to it. It also serves to make the programme more personal.

An interview is driven by the ability/skill of the interviewer. His/her understanding of the topic and background, the research, the kind of questions posed, ability to gauge the reaction of the subject and style determine how great an interview is. The choice of interviewee is important too. What the interviewee has to say, whether it is interesting, whether the interviewee has a valid/interesting point to make (in case the interview forms a part of another programme), the person's ability to communicate eloquently, experiences, attitudes, etc. are factors that contribute to the success of the interview.

The language that is used must be appropriate and the tone and words are determined by the situation and the person(s) being interviewed. The interviewer and/or scriptwriter must keep this fact in mind: while the questions are aimed at the subject, it is being asked for the benefit of the audience. So it must be understandable to the audience. The interview is not a platform for the interviewer to show off his/her knowledge. The questions must be brief, clear and incisive. Active voice and present tense are preferred. The interview must have a focus or an aim and this helps in structuring the content. Some of the questions are pre-planned but a good interviewer has the ability to seize the openings that may arise during the course of the interview and *ask questions off the cuff based on leads or cues in the conversation.* Follow-up questions, too, cannot be pre-planned.

Interviews with the rich and famous (or even ordinary persons who have achieved or done something extraordinary) are popular. *NereChove, Kadhaltuvare, Idavelayil, The Front Row with Anupama Chopra, Tere Mere Beach Mein*, etc. are examples. This format has been copied from the American shows that are highly popular in the US for a long while, with an added Indian touch. The difference though lies in the fact that while we follow the basic interview format, most shows in the US have interviews as a segment in their talk shows, with the hosts inviting and interviewing celebrities, writers, thinkers, politicians, etc.

Film-Based Programmes

Music and films entertain. So it is only natural that they should form a part of TV programming. The fact that such programmes can be executed on a reasonable budget adds to its appeal. Music- and film-based programming can assume many formats.

Reviews on TV are popular music- or film-based programmes. TV is an excellent medium for reviewing film and music as it is possible to include clippings of the film or the video of the music.

A review is an opinion piece by an expert or someone who has considerable knowledge in the field. A good review is a guide for the viewers and helps him/her form a rudimentary idea about the film and reach a decision as to whether he/she wants to watch it.

In the case of a music review, the originality of the piece, how it compares with other pieces of the same genre, quality of voice, emotional resonance, lyrics, style (and whether there has been a change in the artist's or creator's style and rendition), technical quality, whether the video is suitable for the music, etc. are some of the high points of a review.

A good review is always objective and fair and highlights the merits and demerits of the film/music. It is not a venue for the reviewer to vent his/her personal viewpoints, though a review is personal and direct. When the reviewer makes a negative statement he has to justify his/her opinion. The language used in a review must convey action, excitement and drama, without compromising on clarity and credibility. It is normally to have a standard of measurement to rate the film or musical piece. Each reviewer may develop his/her own scale – for example, 4 stars, Thumbs up, Thumbs down, etc.

Phone-in programmes are usually music and film based. Callers can phone in and request that certain songs or clippings from movies to telecast. The anchor/host is an important element in this kind of programming. H/She must be engaging, personable, photogenic, trendy and familiar with the kind of music or films being telecast. The language that is used by the anchor is casual, lively, suitable for the audience and must communicate excitement and vibrancy.

Another kind of programme is one where clippings of film that showcase comedy, action or popular dialogues are shown, for example, *Chirikudukka, Tamasha, Chirikkumthalik, Golden Five*. Theme-based (romance, parental love, heartbreak, family, etc. are just some of the themes) musical programmes, with videos of songs featuring such themes, are shown. Juke-box affords the audience the freedom to select and play songs from the available music list (thumbnails of music videos may be displayed). Programmes like *Chitrahar, Hridayaraagam, Chitrageetham*, etc. are familiar to us and based on music in films.

TV provides scope for musical reality shows like *Indian Voice, Star Singer, Surshetra, Saregama, Indian Idol, Star Voice of India, American Idol*, etc. These reality shows are music based and hugely popular. The contestants, panel of judges, the anchor of the programme all add to the character of the show. Such programmes are normally built on high voltage drama and everything from the judges' comments, personal life of the contestants, their fluctuating fortunes and performances, the set and props, costumes, physical appearances, body language, contestants' performance, rivalries and pettiness that brews backstage – all add to the package.

Documentaries

A documentary is a film that portrays reality. Unlike a film, a documentary is not based on a story that has been conceived in someone's imagination. Nor does it deal with the fantastic or unreal extraordinary. It explores reality and through the images presents a story based on reality or a point of view. The drama in a documentary comes not from the contrived and the manipulated, rather from the drama that is inherent in life and reality. The supreme purpose of the documentary is the representation or recital of the theme.

Documentaries can be on a variety of topics. Wildlife documentaries are extremely popular. It may also be based on events, incidents, people, places, sports or any topic that may be interest to the audience.

Making a documentary demands a special set of skills. The editor and/or maker (the two could be one and the same person and in fact, this is the ideal situation) has an important role to play in how a documentary pans out and how it narrates the story. As it is shot *in situ*, it does not have the security of a script or the controlled environment of a studio set to fall back upon.

Docudrama is a genre of documentary. Here events (especially historical events) are enacted so as to give the audience a better understanding of how something unfolded.

The creator and/or editor decide the course and fate of a documentary. It is essentially an editor's product. Various clippings, sequences of events, interviews are pieced together with narration, music and sound forming the cohesive elements. The documentary maker allows the film to move forward by carefully piecing together various sequences and using a variety of techniques. Narration, and thus language, is dictated by the purpose for the documentary.

The purpose of narration is to engage the audience, to explain, correlate and propel the story forward. The language used must be at once authoritative without being condescending but engaging at the same time. Questions are used sparingly and then only to engage the audience. If questions related to issues or viewpoints are raised, the documentary maker must take the effort to satisfactorily answer the same. On the other hand, the documentary can make an objective portrayal of facts and allow the audience to draw their own conclusions. Statements and opinion are used predominantly. ***Present tense and active voice is preferred. The use of present tense helps bring the events alive (even a historical documentary) and makes it more personal. It is also a technique of narration that is used to hold the audience.***

Editing a documentary

Editing is of utmost importance in documentary making, as it shapes the piece and determines the impact. The director is often in charge of the script and editing too as the separation of the three creative processes could compromise the quality of the film.

The greatest advantage and the greatest challenge to making documentary films is the fact that there are no plots or story to adhere to. A storytelling based on the usual techniques of introduction of a crisis and crisis resolution does not exist in this case. The documentary maker can explore new ways of editing, presenting information and facts, introducing the various facets of the story.

Chronology is not an issue for the editor. By altering the chronology, he/she is able to tell the story in new and novel ways, determine the pace at which information is being related, forces the audience to look at an issue/event from a new perspective and control or determine the reactions of the audience. For doing this, he/she can resort to techniques like juxtaposition of shots, montage etc., coupled with the dexterous use of sound. In doing so, he/she pushes the boundaries of documentary film making and creates a new language for the expression of uncommon sentiments or realities.

Documentary makers believe that it is only through editing that the story is pieced together or that the purpose as well as the meaning of the film emerge. Until it has been skilfully crafted together by editing, the film remains merely a sequence of shots that does not fulfil the task of communicating eloquently.

The editor brings the documentary together based on his/her creative vision. Where a cinema is a director's product, the documentary is essentially an editor's creation.

Apple's Final Cut Studio, Avid, Adobe Premier, Cine Paint Renderman, Sony Vegas, Maigix Video Pro are some of the software used for editing.

Activity: Watch Anand Patwardhan's *A Narmada Diary* and note down the form and technique of narrative, sequences, etc. Comment on the usage of interview footage, shots and logic in narration. Also note how it is different from a commercial or a feature film.

Programmes for National and Rural Development

Various experiments in TV programming have proved that TV can contribute substantially to rural and national development. This is essentially because of the nature of the medium. It is a democratic medium and can be accessed today by a large population, transcending socio-economic barriers. The fact that it does not demand literacy, merely the knowledge of spoken language and the ability to hear and compute information makes it an excellent medium to convey messages to the masses, especially in the rural areas. The fact that it is an audio-visual medium poses another advantage. Concepts that are new or foreign and cannot be adequately expressed through words or which are better communicated through a visual depiction may be easily conveyed through TV. Two decades ago concepts such as polio vaccination, scientific farming and harnessing of water resources were new concepts. TV helped to popularize these concepts or made it acceptable (over a period of time) to rural populace. A demonstration also raises the credibility of the idea being conveyed. When the message is conveyed by a trustworthy source, it becomes more acceptable. Experiments such as the SITE, UGC Model Class, etc. are examples of programmes that target rural and national development. The language used in such programmes is simple, conversational and where possible, mirroring the style and cadence of rural art forms (as these are familiar and acceptable). It must be highly persuasive and must convey facts in an interesting and entertaining manner.

Roles of an Editor and Output Editor

The editor and the output editor are both responsible for the broadcast of a programme. These are the designations that are associated with the production of news and other programmes. The editor assumes a responsible role, as the successful telecast of the programme is dependent on him/her. H/She has overall charge of a programme and is ultimately responsible for every action or decision taken and for the quality of the programme aired.

Where news stories are concerned, they are selected, prioritized, edited and broadcast on the say of the editor. H/She is a creative artist; the content, tone and method of presentation must meet with his/her approval. H/She supervises, controls and mentors every single member in the team. Allocation of duties and assignments falls under his/her purview. H/She must be able to control his/her team and get the best out of each member. In some cases, the editor may even double as the output editor for a shift.

The **output editor** is responsible for the instalment/edition of the programme that he/she is engaged in, during his/her watch, though he/she is answerable to the editor. The output editor looks into selection of news and the lead story, assign stories to reporters, make a call on which stories to continue pursuing and running, determine who to interview for various stories, oversee the technical aspects of the telecast, ensure that the news is logically presented and well structured, that it is balanced, fair and truthful, in keeping with the style of the channel and that it is suitable for telecast. Though both the editor and the output editor are involved in the same job, there is a difference in the level of responsibility shouldered and authority that each possesses.

Exercises

1. Script a feature on one of the following topics:
    a. Kerala as a tourist destination
    b. Tribute to a legendary Indian musician
    c. A Western music composer or singer
    d. FC Barcelona
2. Create a script for a TV drama along the following lines:
    A courtroom – a man has been wrongly accused of murder – young lawyer trying to prove his client's innocence – examining so-called witnesses...
    Create a fitting climax.
3. Take an episode from a reality TV show. Critically examine it to discover the elements that were introduced to ensure its appeal and what contributes to its popularity. Can the elements that are present in a film or drama be seen in it? If yes, how was it introduced?
4. Study an episode from your favourite crime serial or show. Critically analyse it. What does it reveal about the characters? What elements worked? What was the mood, tone? Now write a scene for the same show in keeping with the premise and mood of the show.
5. Take a current episode from your favourite soap or serial or drama and compare it with an episode of same show from Season 1. Analyse changes in characterizations.
6. Write a TV script for a national news bulletin. Duration: 5 minutes. Choose current news stories. Prioritize in order of importance. The script must contain at least one international, national, regional, political and sports news each.
7. Create a video of the same with newscaster or reader reading out the news. Include clippings, graphics, etc.

8. Develop an idea for a special feature based on a festival (Onam, Christmas, Eid, etc.)
9. Write a script for a scene from a TV drama based on the following theme:
   A group of people who meet regularly in secret.
10. Sketch a scene for a comedy. Use humour. Resolve conflict.
    Two characters are at odds with each other.

FILM

Introduction

From its very first exhibition, the motion picture has been a source of wonder and fascination for man. The possibility of telling tales through more than mere narration, through a combination of dialogues, sounds, music, action and more, brought about a new possibility of engaging and entertaining the audience. It provides close to two hours of entertainment, transports viewers from the cinema halls/theatres to a fictional world/reality or to realities different from one's own and elicits a gamut of emotions.

Today, the global film industry is huge, churning out numerous films every year and worth billions. The expenses that have to be borne are outset by the possibility of gaining rich dividends. It is also a media that promises to never go out of style, as long as there are new tales to be told and new worlds or frontiers to explore.

Stages in Filmmaking

The different stages of film making can be broadly divided into **Preproduction, Production and Postproduction.**

Preproduction is the primary stage. The beginning of the film lies in the story idea. The writer/creative artist comes up with an idea that can be communicated visually and this idea is pitched to a director/producer/production house. Sometimes the ideation, screenplay writing and direction are done by the same person. Once the story has been accepted and a contract has been issued, the screenplay is developed. Based on the script, the director (if h/she is not already in the picture) and the crew are hired. The crew would consist of an Art Director and Assistants, Cinematographers, Cameramen, Lighting and Sound technicians (Sound engineers and recordist), Production Assistants and Coordinators, Designers, Script Supervisors, etc. The locations must be identified and arranged for, studio space must be negotiated, transport and accommodation arranged and the filming schedule prepared. Sets must be built, contracts with the various associations and guilds negotiated and signed. In case the film includes visual effects, technicians for the same must be hired. Music is another important component and arrangements must be made for the same.

The actual shooting, referred to as **Production**, happens when all these factors click into place. Once the cameras roll, production begins. It is an expensive process and the preproduction phase is a prerequisite to the smooth execution of the activities in this phase. The director and the cinematographer constantly check the *rushes* to determine the quality and ascertain that the film adheres to the standard and is shaping up in the manner they envisioned. At the end of each day's shoot the film (*workprint)* is sent to the laboratory for necessary processing.

This is followed by Postproduction, where the film begins to emerge in its final shape and form.

- During this phase, the film is edited (shots are selected, placed in sequence, edited together so that there is intelligibility and flow in narration).
- The story must unfold bit by bit. The audience must not be told more than what is necessary.
- Tension, crisis and action are elements that make the film interesting. Humour and emotions may also be used to spice up the narration.
- Editing is a process that brings together these elements in a manner that is appealing and unusual.
- The shooting script is the document that the editor relies upon.

- The director's and the screenplay writer's vision of the film is documented in the form of shots and sequences of scenes, which are numbered.
- The editor relies on this numbering system to weave or edit the film together.
- The first draft that is produced is called the ***rough cut* or the *first cut*.**
- The ***rough cut*** provides an excellent understanding of what the final version will look like. Edited versions that come later are called ***fine cuts***.
- Sound must be mixed with the film. Sound in films consists of dialogues, background sounds and music.
- The sound track is edited and then mixed or synchronized with the film track.
- The film and the sound must be in sync. The *fine cuts* emerge after further editing into the ***final cut.***
- This is the ready-to-print version and the prints meant for distribution are made from this.
- Once the prints are ready for distribution, it is handed over to the distributors, who will have contracts with various cinema halls in place. In keeping with the contracts, the films are exhibited.

Screenplay

The script of a film is called a screenplay. It is the blueprint of a film and provides detailed description of what is seen and heard on the screen.

The origin/source of the story idea and the logline which encapsulates the basic theme is portrayed in the screenplay. The idea must be original or it could be an old/heard tale told in a hitherto untold manner. The screenplay writer/producer/director may also be the source of the story idea. The basic idea must be transformed into a tale that maybe told visually through the medium that is film – a medium that makes demands of its own.

The screenplay writer may either be commissioned to develop the idea or may develop the idea on his/her own with the intention of selling the same to an interested party/production house. The first script that is developed is the spec script/spec screenplay, which differs from the shooting script by virtue of the fact that it contains no shot or production details. A screenplay is prepared before the production begins and is more detailed than spec script and will describe the action, elements that contribute to atmosphere/ambience, dialogues, setting, etc.

A screenplay is written in a standardized format. Hollywood screenplays are written in Courier 12 and usually one page of script translates to one minute of screen time. As a norm, Hollywood screenplays do not go beyond 120 pages. Anything above this is considered long and unacceptable. Indian films, including many regional films, however, are longer and include song (and dance) sequences that increase the length and convey the story in a manner that is different from the Hollywood. Needless to say the not-over-120 pages is not a consideration for Indian films.

To write a screenplay, one has to be a creative artist and a technician who understands the requirements of the medium.

The screenplay is typed with margins on all sides. It uses certain vocabulary in the *Scene Heading*, which places the action in proper context. Before we venture into the learning the format of a screenplay, let's take a look at the terms used:

- INT - Denotes interior and clues in the reader of the script to the fact that the scene is to be shot inside.
- EXT - Denotes exterior; used for scenes shot outside.
- DAY/NIGHT - Places the time of the action at morning or night.
- POV (Point of View) - Denotes whose point of view is being represented or whose view the scene is shot from.
- FADE - Dissolve indicating a slow fade in or fade out (transition from blank screen to scene or vice versa) from the screen. It indicates a major change in story such as passage of time.
- OS (Off Screen) - Speaker is not present in the scene.
- OTS (Over-the-Shoulder Shot) - In this, the back of a person's head and perhaps even one shoulder is shown.
- OC (Off Camera) - The speaker is not present in the scene but not shown on camera.
- CUT TO - Change from one scene to the next instantly.

- CU (Close-Up) - A tightly framed shot of a single person (or object). CU extends from above the head to the upper chest.
- ECU (Extreme Close-Up) - It is used to focus on a single feature of a person or object.
- BCU (Big Close-Up) - This shot shows the entire head.
- MCU (Medium Close-Up) - A bust shot.
- LS (Long Shot) - An establishing shot which includes the whole body of the person, any adjacent persons and the background. It provides a view of the person in relation to the background or a panoramic view of the setting.
- MS (Medium Shot) - It extends from above the head to around the waist or knee and could include a second person.
- B.g. - Background.
- F.g. - Foreground.
- M.O.S (mit out sound) - Shot without sound
- V.O. (Voice Over) - This indicates that the speaker is narrating the action onscreen.
- Pan - Here the stationary camera pivots back and forth or up and down and using this technique captures the scene.
- SFX - Indicates sound effects.
- SPFX - Special effects.

The ***scene heading*** is followed by the description, which briefly describes the 'who' and the 'what'. Who is seen on the screen (and a sense of the character or characters) and what that person is doing is evident from the description. Initially, it is important to give a physical description of the main characters, but in subsequent scenes descriptions may be done away with.

EXT. OUTSIDE CLUB Q'S DUNGEON - NIGHT.
The road is partially lit up by the orange of the streetlights shining a way off. DAMIEN, early 1930s, tall, dark-haired, dangerous looking, looks like a Russian, makes his way through crowd towards the doors of Q's Dungeon. Crowd parts for him. Stops to consult the bouncers.

DAMIEN
(nods)

Busy night!

BOUNCER 1

It is.

DAMIEN
Q in?

BOUNCER 1

Yeah! And asking for you. Wants you to head straight down to the *Cell.*

DAMIEN
(a smirk appears)

Ok.

BOUNCER 1

Cell. Only Q would name his office 'the Cell'!

Points to note about the format

- Scene descriptions must denote when and where the action takes place.
- The names of characters are typed in CAPS.
- If you wish to convey something extra (action/reaction), then it can be added below the name of the character. For example, a smirk appears, smiling, laughing, snorts, etc. There is no space between the name and description.
- The text should be typed leaving margins on all sides.
- The name is usually indented 2.5 inches to the right from the left margin.
- The dialogue is indented right too, though not as far as the name of the character.

Points to note while writing

- The instruction must be descriptive and vivid; it must be clear.

- The idea and writer's visual imagining of the same must be communicated *succinctly* to the director/production house/ technicians.
- The dialogues must sound natural and must follow the normal speech patterns.
- Use vocabulary that one would expect from the character(s) being portrayed and must be in keeping with the personality and background of the character(s).
- Use active voice.
- Use appropriate verbs, for example, *Damien **stalked** into the room* sounds more powerful than *Damien **walked** into the room* or *Damien **strolled** into the room.* The first portrays Damien as a powerful character; the second lacks power and makes it tepid and the third implies a relaxed mood.
- Present tense is preferred.
- Present the conflict. The conflict in the story could be an issue or person. The conflict in a film can take the form of an enemy, be it a personal hurdle/challenge that the protagonist must overcome, ideological disagreements, desire, etc. The conflict is what makes the storyline powerful and gripping and propels the story forward. The process of resolution of the conflict, and the successful resolution of the same brings the story to its climax.
- The seed of the crisis in the story is planted in advance or could be hinted at. The language that is used to express potential crisis must impart a sense of urgency and fear/tension. Future tense and modals of possibility can be used.
- When presenting solutions to problems, it is important to convey a surety or a sense of excitement. Here, the use of pithy dialogue, strong verbs and words is paramount.

Screenplay of Kill Bill (2003)
Source: www.sfy.ru/
Note the vocabulary and abbreviations used.

Pitch – A **pitch** is an attempt to sell a screenplay or procure finance for a project. It is an extremely important endeavour as the success of the pitch determines whether the story idea will be translated into a film.

The pitch maybe directed by the screenplay writer at the director or producer or even by a director at the producer or production house. A pitch is usually an oral exercise and normally details the basic story line or theme of the film. An important part of the pitch is the logline.

A **logline** is a one sentence statement about the film. It compresses the basic ideas into one single sentence, which should never be longer than 25 words. Writing a logline is a challenging and important task as the length of the logline is fixed. In Hollywood, it is considered unprofessional (and a dead starter) to have a logline that goes beyond the limit. It is an important aspect of the pitch as it helps to get the message across. The logline communicates the basic theme and the unique aspects of the story. Who is the hero/main character? What is the crisis/conflict? Where is the story headed? Who is the villain? The logline normally touches upon all these and sheds light on how this film is different from the others and why it should be made into a film.

Logline for *Oceans 13* could be:

Gamblers target Las Vegas casino on a revenge mission and rake in millions.

It brings clarity to the pitch. As the film production progresses, the logline help to keep the creative crew focussed on the plot of the story and discounts the question of digressions.

Where the language of a logline is meant to be descriptive but extremely brief, the pitch (delivered orally) is meant to descriptive, pithy and persuasive. Write visually, in such a manner that the words create pictures in the mind's eye. The pitch must also detail those elements of the film that make it different and saleable. What is the basic plot; who are the main characters (along with brief descriptions about them); how will the story develop (the events that thrust the movie forward); what kind of film is this (funny, romantic, action, etc. so that the mood of the film can be established); target audience (which group is it aimed at/will it be popular with) and budget – the pitch must touch upon these areas and successfully answer questions along these lines.

Exercise: Create loglines for the following films:

1. *The Silence of the Lambs* (1991)
2. *One Flew over the Cuckoo's Nest* (1975)
3. *The Lord of the Rings: Two Towers* (2002)

Features of Dialogue

The language used in films is simple, easy to understand and suitable to the character who 'speaks' the dialogue. The rules of grammar are not strictly followed and the screenwriter has the freedom to break grammatical rules when framing. The only objective is that the intelligibility must not be affected.

- Short sentences are used in screenplays.
- Sentences are usually connected together using simple linking words such as *and*.
- Often the subject of the sentence may be missing altogether and this is acceptable. (*Will do that for you*). Both the subject and the object can be avoided (*Will do that*).
- Sentences may be incomplete and part of the verb dropped (*You kidding?*).
- Things may be left unsaid and the writer can depend on implied meaning to pass the information (*Destroy them!* The audience knows that the '*them*' implied here is the enemy).
- Repetition is used to stress and to make things clear. (*You dare do this to Karl? My best friend Karl?*)
- Dialogues are littered with popular pulp and cultural references (*I dined with the Ratpack!*).
- Pauses, silences are used in conversations to make it believable, to draw attention to specific information and to give the audience time to notice something on the screen and process information. They also make the dialogue more natural.
- Sounds like *hmmm, grr, poof*, etc. are used to lend it realism.
- Stress and intonation is used to convey different shades of meaning, to communicate hesitation, to imply, invite information, etc. [*I* feel that way (pause). Don't *you*? (softly and hesitatingly)]

Things to avoid in dialogue writing

- Long and complex sentences. This is difficult to process.
- Sentences that give out too much information or present information in a convoluted manner must be avoided. Short sentences are preferred.
- Passive verbs must be avoided. They lessen the intensity and affect impact.

To present information in dialogues many literary devices can be used. They are:

- Characterization: this is one manner in which information can be presented. By bestowing certain traits or characteristics on individuals, writers can 'describe' them. (Batman, Joker in *Batman* series)
- Foreshadowing: where the writer hints at what is going to happen.
- Foil: presenting a character who is the antithesis of the protagonist (Draco Malfoy as opposed to Harry Potter)
- Juxtaposition: To place two things side by side to allow comparison or to efficiently present information.
- Flat character: with only one remarkable or noteworthy characteristic or someone who is one-dimensional.

Note: *The examples given below have been written in a style that is acceptable for a movie dialogues and hence may not comply with rules of traditional grammar.*

To add new information transition devices such as the following can be used:

- Moreover (*Monroe is* the *authority on the subject. He is on the board of directors at the museum. Moreover, he is willing to help*).
- Furthermore (*This route takes us through the desert. They won't be expecting us to take it. Furthermore, it's the shortest route and we save time*).

- In addition (*We stake out the place. Try to sit at the next table. Listen for any clues. In addition {pause} we have a great dinner*).
- In addition to (*Durant has a penthouse in the Big Apple, in addition to the Miami Beach house and the condo in Florida*).
- Also (*He is a computer whizkid. He is also a hacker*).
- As well as (*He is an artist as well as a conman*).
- Another (*He is likely to be elected. He has contributed much to the nation. Another point in his favour is the fact that his opponent is unpopular*).

Showing Contrast

- On one hand (*I don't know what to believe. On the one hand he shows all signs of wanting to jump on board on the other there is all the information about him that indicate he is not a team player*).
- However (*I thought you would grab the opportunity. However, you seem uninterested*).
- Nevertheless (*The thought of being polite to that incompetent fool galls me. Nevertheless, the situation demands it*).
- Still (*You are not ideal for the role, still, do we have a choice?*).
- But (*Love the idea but it's not doable at this point*).
- Yet (*The trail seems easy enough, yet its known to be a dangerous path*).
- Although (*Although we have the codes for the safe, that alone will not get us through*).
- While (*While he is simple, he is no man's fool*).

Showing Cause and Effect

- Hence (*The summons have come. Hence, I must leave*).
- Because (*I couldn't come to you because I was needed here. My family needed me. The ranch needed me.* The same sentence can be put in another way, excluding the 'because', to show cause and effect. *I couldn't come to you. I was needed here. My family needed me. The ranch needed me*).
- Thus (*He was in a horrific car crash. Thus, he was paralysed*).

- Therefore (*He is going. Therefore, so must I*).
- Due to (*I was delayed, due to those unforeseen events. It wasn't my fault*).
- Can cause (*Don't get too close to the machine. It can cause you serious harm*).
- Consequently (*He was betrayed. Consequently, he was arrested*).

Activity

- Watch the film *Step Up* (2006). Analyse the dialogues (first 15 minutes) to identify the peculiarities in the conversation. Note change in vocabulary induced by culture, age, social factors.

Language in Films

Addition of in-vogue vocabulary, genre specific

Where newspapers comply with traditional standards of language, the broadcast media and film are more flexible and ready to accept the changes in vocabulary and incorporate new words into the schema of the film. In fact, the vocabulary of films is constantly adapting and changing to accommodate the changes that language is constantly undergoing. Along with vocabulary, the changes in style, manner of speaking, speech patterns and rhythms are incorporated. This acceptance and change is necessary to lend the characters credibility and place them within the requisite social, demographic and cultural contexts. Such changes are more evident in coming-of-age films and in films that deal with subjects related to youth.

A change that is evident is the manner in which language is used. Contracted forms are a norm now; whereas an analysis of the English language films of the 1950s and 1960s will reveal the use of traditional sentence structures, complete with prepositions and articles. In-vogue form of language does not use complete sentences, prefers contracted forms and drops prepositions, connectors and articles. The language is reminiscent of the form that is used in SMS and this is natural as it is being imitated in speech as well. Films also use new currency vocabulary and phrases. It is not uncommon to hear such dialogues as *He's a jerk and a hothead* or *What a screw up!*

Language changes with genre. It plays a unique role in conveying emotions and adding depth to the scene. A thriller/action adventure film uses words that denote action and which convey urgency, strength of purpose, which communicates the strong/passionate thoughts/ideology of the characters and explain their motivation. The following dialogue conveys a sense of finality and certain doom (for the enemy).

> "The age of Men is over. The time of the Orc has come."
> *Lord of the Rings: Return of the King (2003)*

Some well-known/popular dialogues from Hollywood

- "I'll be back." (*The Terminator*, 1984)
- "I'm gonna make him an offer he can't refuse." (*The Godfather*, 1972)
- "Keep your friends close, but enemies closer." (*The Godfather II*, 1974)
- "May the force be with you." (*Star Wars* series)
- "Bond. James Bond." (Bond series)
- "Here's looking at you kid." (*Casablanca*, 1942)
- "I think this is the beginning of a beautiful friendship." (*Casablanca*, 1942)
- "Of all the gin joints, in all the towns, in all the world, she walks into mine." (*Casablanca*, 1942)
- "Frankly, my dear, I don't give damn." (*Gone with the Wind*, 1939)
- "*They* may take our lives, but they'll never our freedom." (*Braveheart, 1995*)

Westerns are littered with phrases and vocabulary which are quintessentially American and Western in character and unique to the genre. They lend character and believability to the scene and character(s) as the language reflects the personality of the land and the people.

Examples

- "These injuns smell a little gamey, Captain. They rub skunk oil on themselves to keep off bugs and flies." (*Distant Drums,* 1951)
- "They still don't like fightin' at night. But they'll come a hootin' and a hollerin' at dawn!"(*Distant Drums*, 1951)
- "You ain't gettin' no older than tomorrow." (*One-Eyed Jacks*, 1961)
- "Don't say it's a fine morning or I'll shoot ya" (*McLintock*, 1963)
- "When a man with a .45 meets a man with a rifle, you said the man with the pistol's a dead man. Let's see if that's true." (*A Fistful of Dollars*, 1964)
- "Young fella, if you're looking; for trouble I'll accommodate ya." (*True Grit*, 1969)
- "Are you going to pull those pistols or whistle Dixie?" (*The Outlaw Josey Wales*, 1976)

Film Themes

Films reflect the mores, values and culture of a society and have sometimes been accused of shaping and creating a new set of values, validating foreign values and forcing or infusing undesirable changes in society.

While the latter opinion is a source of much debate, there is no doubt that films are a form of social commentary and sometimes make a more accurate assessment of and take a more brutally honest look at the society that they portray.

The tapestry of Indian social life is often laid bear through cinema, as may be witnessed in *Ankur, Prem Rog, Ek Chadar Maili Si, Tamas, Salaam Bombay!, Sadak, Maachis, Sardari Begum, Water, Kanchivaram, A Wednesday, Gangs of Wasseypur* etc. Gender inequalities and social injustice are eloquently discussed. Cases in point are *Mother India, Ankur, Aakrosh (1980), Nikaah, Saaransh, Damini, Bandit Queen, Astitiva, Kya Kehna, Lajja, Firaaq, Aarakshan* and *Papilio Budhha.*

Films often make statements about the political situation that prevails, the inadequacies or loopholes in the administration of justice and portrays the corruption that pervades society. The supreme advantage that money, power and influence offers over the myth of equality perpetuated by political manifestos and promises is brought to light in films. These ever-popular themes have been portrayed in Indian movies such as *Andhaa Kanoon, Ardh Satya, God and Gun, Black Friday, Raajneeti, Singham* (Tamil and Hindi) etc. Malayalam films such as *Commissioner, Oru Abhibhashakante Diary, The King, Oraal Matram, Lion, Rashtram, Passenger* etc. are also examples of films portraying such themes. Films can be political in character but use satire and a family setting to tell the story. *Sandesham*, scripted by Sreenivasan, is an example.

Nakarame Nandi, Satya, Makalkku, Page 3, Fashion, Subramaniapuram, Ente bring to light the harsh realities of modern life.

Hollywood films like *The Great Dictator, The Great Escape, Schindler's List,* etc. make statements about the situation of its time and provides social and political background information. M.T. Vasudevan Nair's movies are often a commentary on the joint Nair families of Malabar and provide an insight into the community and its ways. Movies like *Pardeesa, PadamOnnu OruVilaapam* comment on the atrocities/injustices/illicit activities that perpetuate in certain communities.

The supreme advantages that money, power and influence offer over the myth of equality perpetuated by political manifestos and promises is brought to light in films such as *Passenger, OruAbhibashakante Diary, OraalMatram,* etc. *Makal* and *Nakarame Nandi* brings to light the harsh realities of modern life.

The acceptance of 'new generation' films reflects the changing expectations from viewers. They deal with issues/tales that hitherto have never been discussed or have been done so in a manner and using language that had been absent from the Indian film scenario. *Kaminey* and *Delhi Belly* are set against the backdrop of the underbelly of society and are known for its profane and crude language. *Ishqiya* and *Dirty Picture* have an unapologetic in-the-face sexuality that is 'new'. The dialogues and characterization contribute to this impression. There are no taboos in speaking about sex, in engaging in elicit professions or engagements. It gives the impression that it is commonplace and not something that can be discussed only behind closed doors. *Dev D* (a modern retelling of the Bengali classic, *Devdas*) and *Vicky Donor* (on sperm donation) can be considered new generation movies. *Dil Chahta Hai, Wake*

Up Sid, *Zindagi Na Milegi Dobara* (coming of age and/or based on the theme of friendship), *Mr. and Mrs. Iyer* (set against the backdrop of communal tensions), *Rang De Basanti* (which promotes political change through force), *Nishabd* and *Cheeni Kum* (which explores the relationship between an older man and a much younger woman) are films that have had mass appeal, yet have been path breakers.

22 Female Kottayam, the 2012 Malayalam movie, talks about a young woman who is in a live-in relationship and who frankly admits that she does not conform to the standards/strictures placed by society. Is this a reflection of the changing concept of womanhood and subversion of mores? One cannot say with any degree of certainty. *Trivandrum Lodge* is blatant in its sexuality and makes no bones about it. The female lead character is shown to be 'liberated' and the female characters are coarse and open in their discussion about sex and that is a change from what was hitherto acceptable in a film.

Exercises

1. Write a scene following these instructions:
   A public building – 4 different characters from different socio-economic backgrounds – characters get stuck in a lift
   Develop a story, write a script. Introduce the element of tension/conflict. Bring out the differences in characterization.
2. Take a popular movie. Write synopsis with changes.
3. Cast characters (with changes in original cast) for a movie of your choice.
4. Write a synopsis of a story based on the lyrics given below. It would be better if the reference were not literal and obvious.

On a dark deserted highway

5. Write a shooting script for one of the following sequences. Imagine the situation, introduce characters. Duration: 90 sec.

A man is murdered in a hotel room.

6. Pick a movie. Download a copy of its screenplay. Watch it, pausing often (preferably after every scene). Write a description for every scene. Now, compare it to the original screenplay. What did you miss? Notice how the story or main plot and subplot

progresses, characterization, and how elements of humour, terror, horror, pain etc has been incorporated, psychological aspects, if any etc. Write a report on the basis of your analysis.

7. Pick a movie of your choice. Note the story line and write a synopsis. Change the climax of the movie.
8. Watch *The Good, The Bad, The Ugly* or *Guns of Navarone.* Choose one scene and list each shot in it. Identify camera angles (CU, MS, LS, etc.) and camera movements (zoom, pan, dolly, tilt) and descriptions of action occurring in the scene. Use the given example from *The Seven Samurai* as format for the exercise.

Scene: Heihachi's Funeral

The Samurai bury Heihachi after he dies during a raid. The farmers and Samurai mourn his loss. The wild Kikuchiyo galvanizes the village with Heihachi's flag. At that moment, bandits attack that village.

Low-angle, Long shot of the hillside. Encircled by villagers, the Samurai bow before Heihachi's grave mound. The wind blows.

Low-angle, Medium long shot of Samurai. This a zoomed shot at the same angle – the Samurai perform the burial ritual.

Low-angle, Medium long shot of Kikuchiyo, framed left. This is an even closer view, same angle. The camera tracks Kikuchiyo as he plunges Heihachi's sword into his grave, then sits, despondent.

Return to Low-angle, Long shot of the hillside. The Samurai and farmers kneel before Heihachi's grave mound.

9. Write a script for a chase scene. The villains are pursuing the hero or heroine. The hero/heroine is unaware of why he/she is threatened. Show his/her panic, confusion, etc. Develop story.
10. Observe the people around you. Pick out one unique or novel characteristic about an individual. Now create a fictional character that possesses this unique characteristic and write the outline of a story about them.
11. Write a screenplay based on the following. Include twists and cliffhangers. Create a climax, which resolves the conflict that you introduced.

    It's late. The heroine is tired. She lives in a flat which has minimal security. The light goes out.
12. Write a story and screenplay based on any one of the following:

a. Fulfilling dreams
b. Lost Antique Key
c. A Secret

13. Identify the social issues discussed in any five recently released movies of your choice.

CHAPTER 4

Digital Media

Introduction

According to Young, (Young M.L. 2009. *Internet Millenium*. New Jersey: Prentice Hall) the Internet may be defined as 'a network of networks that connects computers all over the world.' It is a super network that contains all sorts of information and is called the information highway.

Young also points out that these networks consist of not only the hardware aspects but the software as well.

The hardware is made up of the computer, modem, cable, satellite, etc. while the software allows for exchange of information through protocols.

Characteristics of the Internet

- Connects communities that are spread across the globe, breaking down physical, political, social and cultural barriers.
- Helps in free exchange of thoughts, ideas and data.

- A forum for social interactions, involving email, chat, messaging and more. It is an electronic medium and a social space.

While the Internet is the communication network or information network, the WWW is one of the services that make use of the internet. Tim Berners-Lee invented the World Wide Web. It is like an encyclopaedia, a telephone directory, a record collection, a video shop and a speakers' Corner, all combined and accessible through any computer. Through its increased usage, the term is sometimes used interchangeably with the Internet, but the two are different entities.

Digital Media – Some Forms

Digital media has global reach and allows instant access and quick reproduction. The bywords of digital media are interactivity, hypertext and virtuality.

E-books

Electronic books are simply defined by the *Oxford Dictionary of English* as '*an electronic version of a printed book*'. In other words, while a conventional book is made of paper and printed using ink, the e-book is an electronic form of the same, which uses neither paper nor ink. The first electronic book was the Sony Bookman which was introduced in the market in 1991. Rocket eBook of Gemstar/NuvoMedia and the Peanut Reader of Peanut Press were some of the other e-books brought out in the late 90s. The most popular e-Readers, the hardware part of an e-Book, are Amazon Kindle, Sony Reader, BeBook, etc.

E-newspaper

An e-newspaper (online newspaper or web newspaper) has an online presence or it exists only on the internet. They contain a digitalized blend of text, photos, graphics, audio and video.

Examples of traditional newspapers with online presence:

Newspapers like *The Hindu* (thehinduonline.com), *The Indian Express* (indianexpress.com), *The New Indian Express* (expressbuzz.com), *The New York Times*, *Los Angeles Times* (TimesLink), *Chicago Tribune*, etc. provide news through their websites.

Online-only papers do not have printed copies and are available only as soft copies. Examples: *The Santiago Times* which operates out of Santiago, Chile is a pure e-newspaper. *South Park Reporter* (a weekly regional paper from UK, established in 2000); *Seattle Post-Intelligencer* (which became an online only newspaper in 2009 after publishing in hard print for 149 years), *Caledonian Mercury, etc.*

There are some newspapers however which are principally online newspapers, but publish a few printed copies. For example, annarbor.com brings out hard copies bi-weekly.

E-magazines

Electronic magazines (also called e-zines or webzines or cyberzine or hyperzine) are the electronic versions of print magazine or magazines that can be only accessed online. *The National Geographic* and *Newsweek* have online as well as print versions. *Slate* and *salon.com* have been designed specifically for web consumption. Online magazines may be accessed free of cost or you may have to pay a subscription fee.

Characteristics of E-magazines

- E-zines are normally shorter than the traditional magazine as it is not easy to read online for long periods of time.
- The type and the font facilitate easy reading.
- Similar or related points are chunked together.
- Subheads are used as it helps readers scan through the article easily.
- It features a variety of articles including interviews, profiles, human interest stories, features, recipes, travelogues, etc.
- It provides a completely different experience as it uses graphics, video and audio files.

E-journal

E-journals or electronic journals are journals of any nature that are broadcast or accessed via an electronic media. The term normally refers to journals that are published on the internet or the web. They can be downloaded. But as these are normally scholarly publications, they might not be available from the sellers of e-books.

- E-journals are normally meant for academic learning and research.
- The format of e-journal closely follows that of traditional journals.
- Some e-journals offer limited access to its pages. Such journals allow the user to browse through and view a few pages. Access to the article in its entirety will be limited and will be allowed only after the user has paid the access or subscription fee.

Writing for the Web

Guidelines, planning, structure and style

When you start writing for the web the first thing that you ought to remember is that people read differently on the web. Reading on a screen is physiologically more difficult than reading on paper. Reading for a long time on a screen makes your eyes hurt; it is laborious and also time consuming.

How web users read

- They scan pages.
- They prefer to read chunks of information.
- They move from one link to another searching for newer and different information.
- When the content is very long most readers prefer to take a print out and read.

Conventional style of writing follows a pyramid style. It provides background information quotes many sources and moves towards a logical conclusion. When you write in this style you are demanding that your readers do a lot of reading to get top the core of the matter. This is not the way to write for the web.

Good web writing follows the inverted pyramid style, which is borrowed from journalism.

When writing for the web

- Make sure that you hook the reader in the beginning itself.
- Convey one idea in one paragraph.
- Start with the conclusion, provide the details in the following paragraphs. Front-loading content means starting with the conclusion followed by the what, how, where, when and why. The first line of each paragraph should contain the conclusion for that paragraph, so that readers can immediately understand what the paragraph is about and decide if they want to read the rest of the paragraph or the page or not.
- Remember to answer the 5 Ws and H.
- Cut out the dead wood. Use half the number of words you would when you write for the print media. It is quite irritating for readers scroll down often. Hence make your copy short.
- Write in such a way that you will be easily found in a search. Optimize the content for the search engines.
- Be clear, concise and direct.
- Use the active voice.
- Use hyperlinks and allow the user to navigate away from the page. This provides a change and relieves the monotony of reading for a long time on screen.
- Highlighting, underlining, use of italics and bold increases the readability.
- Use the method of *chunking* (where all references to an idea or point or references made by a person are 'chunked' or placed together in a single paragraph). Then the reader does not have to go back and forth between pages to clarify information.
- When writing for the web, complete sentences are not always necessary. But avoid telegraphic writing. Omitting articles such as

"the" or "a" to shorten a sentence only makes the sentence more difficult to read.
- Resort to the 'blocking' technique, whereby all references or quotes of a particular person are put into a single block.
- Use a bulleted list if there is a scope for itemization or if many related facts are mentioned.
- Avoid jargon or complicated terms. Use simple language.
- Invite user participation in the form of blogs, comments or messages.
- Include name and contact information at the end/beginning of the copy.

Headlines and Blurbs

These form the 'microcontent' of an article. A single webpage may exhibit varied and sometimes unrelated stories. The headline and the blurb offer information about the article and the reader can decide whether or not to read the story.

Headline

Use a different font, colour and size for the headline. This will create a visual hierarchy to your web page which facilitates online reading. Remember these points while framing your headline:

- It must be attention grabbing.
- It should focus on the main point of the story.
- It is brief.
- It has important information or keywords at the beginning.
- Use active and strong verbs.

Blurbs

Blurbs are pieces or comments that clarify the headline and give information on the story that accompanies it. They are normally found below the headline and simplify it. A blurb can also be a teaser or a lead-in to a news story. It determines whether the user is going to click on the link page and read on or move on.

- It is short and comprises up to 40 words.
- It is clear.
- It gives a brief picture about the important features of the story.
- The style is simple and not obtuse.
- The first paragraph(s) or **Lead** is an important part of the web article. It must include the most important details of the story or article. It normally follows the five Ws and one H pattern (Who, What, Where, When, Why and How). You can use the types of leads mentioned in newspaper writing.
- While writing for the web you can also use:
  (i) *List leads* that provide a range of related facts. It can be followed by a nut/focus paragraph that clarifies the connection between the facts.
  (ii) *Delayed identification lead that* does not identify the person in the story immediately. it can be used when the person is not well known and the subject matter is more important than the person.

Web Copy

When a sales message appears on the web, the text of the advertisement is called web copy. Web copy is different from web content – web copy has a selling aspect; web content is primarily information for informing, educating or entertaining readers.

The web copy has the same objectives any advertising message – to attract attention, gain interest in the product, educate the user and persuade them to buy.

Challenges in writing web copy

Though relatively cheap, it is a highly competitive medium. Web users surf from one site to the next and scan each page in a matter of seconds.

So the ad has to attract the attention of the reader and the message must register quickly.

- Write the way you speak – easy, informal and conversational.
- Provide information.
- Use colloquialism. It brings informality and ease to the copy.
- Avoid use of jargon. It creates frustration and resentment.
- Use testimonials – it adds credibility to the advertising message.
- Copy should inspire trust. This is a valuable asset, especially on the net.
- Include an option for soliciting visitors' names and email ids.
- Try to get feedback from customers. For example an astrology site would give the user the option of receiving weekly newsletters, astrological profiles, updates, etc. This way it can try to sell services and inform subscribers about discounts, special offers, etc.
- Copy must contain 'meta keywords' (terms relevant to the topic) so that the link comes up during web search.

Profile Writing

Profiles are full-length commentaries or vignettes of people and slices of their life. It must be a revealing and interesting story about the subject and include details like background, interests, ambitions, passions, struggles, etc.

Profiles are biographical and written from the perspective of the subject. A good profile is one that gives the reader a fair idea about the person, his/her attitudes, personality, habits and more.

The heart and soul of a profile is in the interview. Profiles are the result of one or a series of interviews, at least one of them intense. Where an interview is an excerpt from a conversation that you have with the subject, the profile includes the same but more. The profile is not written over a day but may take weeks to compile as it requires input from numerous sources.

- Once you have been given the assignment, research on the subject.

- Decide on the focus of the profile and thus the focus of the interview(s).
- Interview the subject, family, friends, colleagues, etc.
- Brief the subject beforehand on questions that are likely to be asked.
- Make the subject comfortable. Persuade them to share little known facts or interesting personal information and anecdotes.
- Observe keenly – their mannerisms, facial expressions, sense of humour, etc. This will add to the 'feel' of the article.
- Follow-up interviews have to be arranged if you need to gather more information.

When writing the profile

- Create visuals with words and bring the subject alive in the minds of the reader.
- Use quotes or excerpts from dialogues with the subject and other sources.
- Include details that the average reader wants to know.
- Give the reader reason to feel that the subject is worth reading about.

Profiles must be accompanied by excellent photographs that add to the tone and feel of the profile and provide a visual glimpse into the person and his/her life.

Blogs

Web logs or blogs, as they are commonly called, are a type of website that is made up of journal-like entries. It:

- allows freedom of expression.
- facilitates discussions with people who have similar and related interests.
- acts as a source of information and news.

Kinds of blogs

Personal blogs

- Focuses on an individual's life opinions and beliefs.
- May or may not give bloggers the option to post their comments.

Interest- or topic-based blogs (hobbies, professions, etc.)

- May be run by communities or by a group of collaborators.
- Shares new information, ideas and provide links to related information.

Filter blogs

- Focuses on the blogger's web experiences.
- Filters the web from the viewpoint of the blogger.
- Some provide only lines of links, often with some commentary.

Layout and structure of blogs

Most blogs have a common layout. Blog posts or the main content is kept in the widest column, while the extra or additional contents like the widgets (code that one can paste onto the blog template that allows one to automatically display one's activity on another site), links, descriptions, titles, etc. may be found around the edges of the page. Blogs can use a combination of text, audio, graphics, photos, video, etc. and carry advertisements.

Blogs are made of numerous posts – the main content. Each post might have a title. The narrow columns on the side may even post links to older posts or the archives, to other blogs or to comments.

- They are written in an informal style.
- Blogs are participatory media as it allows contributions from many individuals.
- Blogs have an automatic archiving system that allows the display of the latest post, with the option of accessing older posts.

- Users must create profiles by provide information about themselves and choosing a 'name' or 'handle'.
- RSS (Really Simple Syndication) alerts users to new content or posts and feeds embedded in other web pages, allowing easy monitoring of content.
- Develop your own style and express your individuality.
- Do not express opinions that are publicly unacceptable or insensitive.
- Write with clarity of purpose.
- Title posts should grab attention, contain keywords/ideas and summarize.
- Use subheads as they help the readers to scan through main points.
- List information where you can.
- Format the content with left-align text; put double break between paragraphs; font should be readable and use font size 10 or 12.
- Formatting (underlining, caps, italics, etc.) should be used to draw the eye.
- Use white space to draw attention to specific parts and to provide aesthetic relief.
- Use links within your posts. This will help not only increase the number of clicks you receive but also help with your blog's search engine rankings.
- Include images. Not all posts will need images, but when they do, take advantage of it.
- Respond to blog comments.

Exercise

Develop a personal blog.

Editing for Digital Media

Editing is the art of polishing copy or content to enhance its value and make it more effective. It is also a process that aims at making the copy error-free and increasing clarity. The rules of editing for web are basically similar to editing for any other media.

Responsibilities of the editor

- The editor must develop a signature style that communicates the personality of the website, and in turn the company, person, organization, etc.
- He/she is responsible for all the contents on the website.
- The editor must develop a procedure to ensure that the material is error-free and updated.
- The editor must check for spelling, grammatical errors, names, designation, punctuation, capitalization, etc. He/she should also arrange related facts 'chunked' together and use bulleted form whenever possible.
- Ensure that the copy is navigable by using navigational cues – change in font size, bold, italics, etc. must be used.
- Check for suitability of photos, graphics, video etc. Edit/change these elements if required.
- Make the webpage highly interactive.

Language Techniques for Search Engine Optimization (SEO)

Search Engine Optimization (SEO) is a technique which helps search engines find and rank your site higher than other similar sites in response to a search. It helps you to get a lot of visitors to your site. Search engines crawl the web, using a particular software, called a 'crawler' or a 'spider'. Spiders follow links and index everything they find. You must check what a crawler sees on your site. Sometimes they might not get the correct meaning of a page. So you have to use such words that will not create any ambiguity.

Website ranking is determined by many factors such as the connection of the search term to the item searched for, use of keywords and phrases within the text, etc.

To ensure SEO

- Try to get established websites related to your area link to your web pages. Links from other websites and blogs help the search engines find you easily.
- Search engines can't 'read' images and animations, so they need informative text. Make sure that you give the search engines reading material that is relevant and sufficient.
- Identify your target market. What are the keywords they are likely to use? Try to adapt to the type of language they are familiar with.
- Make sure that your web page is unique and has an identity.

Writing Effectively for the Social Media

- Pack your writing with energy by using a lot of action words and strong verbs. Steer clear of the usual mundane words.
- Aim for clarity and conciseness. Try putting the information in bullet points. Your writing becomes succinct when you use bulleted points and you don't compromise on clarity either.
- Make sure that what you write is informative as well as engaging.
- Ensure search engine optimization.
- Check for errors.

Podcasting

The word podcast is a portmanteau word that combines broadcast with the word iPod (one of the most popular portable MP3 players developed by Apple).

When you listen to a broadcast you are constrained in your listening as you have to listen to what is played by the jockey. But with the podcast revolution you can create and listen to any kind of audio content that you want.

You don't need specialized knowledge to create a podcast. The subjects on which podcasts are based are wide ranging. People create podcasts on movies, technology, music and even politics. The style used also differs. Some are like talk shows; others merely provide information on current events or trends. Creative people can indulge in their creativity through the medium of podcasts as it is very cheap and has a wide reach. Broadcast regulations have not yet been imposed on this media and hence there are no constraints as such. Podcasts can be downloaded to your computer and synced to your MP3 player automatically. As no effort is required on the listener's part it has become very popular.

Unlike internet streaming audio, you can take a podcast without being tied to a computer as it can be downloaded, paused and played repeatedly.

Unlike the radio where you have to spend a lot of time listening to advertisements most podcasts are commercial-free. The cost of podcasting is low enough for podcasters to air their shows without sponsorship.

You are not bombarded with podcasts like email spam as you get only the podcasts you subscribe to.

So if you are a creative person looking for a channel to showcase your talents this is the right space for you.

Exercise

Develop a podcast based on your favourite music director/composer.

CHAPTER 5

Advertising

Introduction

The world of advertising has witnessed revolutionary changes in its concept, multimodal representation and use of language. The history of advertising reveals that the biggest change has come in terms of content, tone, out lay and in layering it with our lived experiences. Advertising has become a very powerful discourse as it allows us to think about any event or product that it has highlighted critically, using our own perspective.

The greatest challenge of advertising is always to produce an effective ad that has a powerful selling line. Language in advertising plays a very dominant role in eliciting powerful response from the public. Amul's *utterly, butterly delicious* is one of the memorable slogans that has stayed with Indians. The utterly, butterly was pinpointed as ungrammatical, but Sylvester D Cunha decided to go ahead with the caption with the unusual, ungrammatical words which had a special rhyme and gave the brand its longevity. Then in Indian advertising we have Nike's 'Just do It'; MRF's 'The Tyre with Muscle'; Hamara Bajaj; 'Washing Powder Nirma'; 'No One can eat Just One' and so on.

Advertising has become one of the powerful tools for marketing. The main objective of advertising thus becomes challenging. It has to inform and persuade people to buy food, clothing, housing, transportation, entertainment, digital products, etc. closer to dailiness of life which witness vast majority of consumer spending. Drugs, health products and automobiles are also equally important when it comes to consumers. Most of the international and national companies invest huge sums to market their brand. To produce an advertisement that sells is the greatest challenge of the marketing company. David Ogilvy, the most sought after wizard in advertising business points out that the first task is to make the product itself the hero of your advertising. Colourless, insipid writing can become a bad campaign. According to him "… a good advertisement can be thought of as a radar sweep, constantly hunting for new prospects as they come in to the market".

Writing for advertisements is extremely challenging. Language has to be powerful and persuasive. It has to convey the uniqueness of your product and the big idea that you are using to attract the attention of the customers. We now live in a world where people do not have time for long winding reading material and long textual campaigns. Attention span of the consumers has become short. Powerful language, image and setting of an ideal frame will have its own distinct function of conveying specific aspects of an advertisement. It is this multimodal representation that becomes a normal state of communication in an advertisement. The world of advertising has absorbed and reflected a lot radical changes, especially in its representation and language production. These changes are well marked in the new advertisement campaigns in print media to the screen, older technologies of print to digital and in the shift from the dominance given to writing to the dominance given to visual effects, photography and minimalism in language use.

Designing your language is equally important as designing your product representation. Representational and communicational practices are constantly subject to change. They are altered and blended to communicate powerfully. An advertisement becomes very persuasive when it is linked to socially and culturally available resources. It is the cultural milieu that provides the semiotic resource for great ideas. When Hare Krishna Movement became popular in India with their campaign *Hare Rama Hare Krishna - Hare Hare*, Amul immediately responded with *Hurry Amul, Hurry Butter – Hurry, Hurry*!

Elements of Advertising

Advertising is one of the most powerful tools of human communication. It is paid, non-personal form of communication about organization/products/services that is transmitted through mass media. It should be persuasive. Advertisements provide information about the products. The information need not be complete or truthful. The sellers decide the information that they want to share with the consumers. So the information that they use will never highlight the flaws of the product. But this is accepted by the industry, regulators and consumers and is called **puffery**. Exaggeration for effect is accepted as a normal practice in advertising.

Advertising should be persuasive. The consumer products around us demonstrate the divergence. The national and international companies go on introducing new products that force feed the process of divergence. It is a powerful ad that persuades the consumer to identify and differentiate the product from another. Creating a new category and making it different is the essence of success in the advertising field. The concept of establishing a brand may look simple but to establish a bond with the consumers is the task assigned to the advertising agency.

Products, services and ideas are very important to the advertiser. A product is the sum total of social, economic and psychological values that are important to the customer. Creating a breakthrough product to capture the attention of the consumer becomes the task of the advertiser. What is very important in communication is the detailing of the product. You may have only 30 seconds to win your target audience. According to A.G. Krishnamurthy, founder of Mudra Communications, identity and continuity are a brand's pillars. Brands have a life, a unique identity and it transacts with the consumer.

There are a few brands which created a new category and assumed the position of the leader.

Can you identify:

1. The first online book store
2. The first adhesive bandage
3. The first cable sports network
4. The first direct seller of personal computers

5. The first cable news network
6. The first detergent
7. The first weekly news magazine
8. The first plain-paper copier
9. The first men's magazine

Discuss in groups the perception behind the creation of this category. How effective is the perception of leadership in blocking other brands?

The primary objective of advertising is to create an image of the product in the mind of the consumer. The products may not have substantial differences. They are referred to as **parity products**. How to produce advertising that sells depends upon many factors. According to Ogilvy one has to do one's homework. You have to study your product. The greatest challenge for you is to create a unique message that will win your target audience. You have to do a lot of research to create new information from the clamorous information explosion that we are living with. Only research will enable you to identify the strength and weakness of your product.

Language Techniques

Language gains intensity to communicate the deepest emotions. The UK creative powerhouse BBH uses ESP (Emotional Selling Proposition) and has produced some landmark ads. The ads created by Nike for empowerment through sport, Singapore Airline's Girl, De Beers making its products symbol of eternal love, Huggies symbolizing parents' love and Amul ads' deeper engagement with the problems of everyday life in India use language as a springboard to convey powerful emotions. Amul hoardings, especially Billboards like Eek-mail (documenting deadly virus); I-fun (popularity of i-phone) and Face bhook or Utterly Twitterly delicious are ad campaigns were successfully developed using ESP.

Go through the slogans listed below and identify the products:

1. Fresh & Juicy

2. Impossible is nothing
3. Thirsts asks nothing More
4. It's Good To be Home
5. What's the secret of this speed? Ask the master.
6. Express yourself.
7. Live on the coke side of Life
8. Think small
9. Live the rush
10. The best start for today and tomorrow

Slogans use a number of language devices to convey their message. They use personal pronouns, adjectives, action verbs and comparisons to communicate in an emphatic language.

An important part of framing slogans is an awareness how the slogan is organized and the impact of it on the reader. It has to have a resonance. The way you organize your ideas and the linguistic (grammar and vocabulary) choices that you make play a big role in making your slogan powerful as well as memorable Greg Myers (Myers 1997) uses the term 'slogan' for any catchy phrase. In many cases, the boundaries between slogan and headline disappear. An advertising layout is divided into several parts: headline, body copy, signature line (a mention of a brand-name, often accompanied by a price-tag, slogan or trade-mark) and standing details (e.g., the address of the firm). The advertising slogans of the strongest brands have fine tuned their language to the core identity of their brand. For example, cow boy image is associated with Marlboro cigarettes.

Find the powerful by lines of the products and discuss the language use:

1. BMW
2. Coke
3. LUX
4. Kelvinator
5. Raymonds
6. Wills
7. Kit Kat

When we analyse the slogans and the product that they advertise, there may be a few things that we arrive at, as a set of guidelines for a brand's values. Let us list some words to bring out the main output of this session. Honest, confident, understanding, warm, witty (but not offensive) and innovative. These qualities are powerfully conveyed through a language that shapes the destiny of your product. It brings responsibility as well as power, as words are tied to emotions. Advertising is writing ideas. It is hard, as it puts forward to you the greatest challenge to be original. That is why we say 'great advertising happens when creativity and relevance meet'.

Let us look at the language use of the slogans. Geoffrey Leech in his 'English in Advertising: A Linguistic Study of Advertising in Great Britain' writes that the language of advertising belongs can be labelled as 'loaded'. He sets the following principles of advertising texts: Attention value, Readability (by means of simple, personal and colloquial style), Memorability (most important in the process of advertising is to remember the name of the product) and selling.

Let us take a look at a memorable print ad created by Ogilvy for Rolls Royce:

'At 60 miles an hour the loudest noise in this new Rolls Royce comes from the electric clock.'

The main subject is that the car is acoustically tuned and the use of the numeral 60 miles an hour gives an authenticity to the technical efficiency of the automobile. The adjective 'loudest' is used with precision to emphasize that the only sound that the passenger will hear is the ticking sound of the electric clock. The demonstrative pronoun, **this**, functions as an attribute to the fact that the engine is silent.

Here cohesion devices are used effectively to prevent unnecessary repetition in the text. We can pin point another feature for advertising – **cataphora:** first the description of the product and later on the name of the product is mentioned. The sellers create a powerful impression that this is the only product that can offer you something unique.

What do you mean by the term **cohesion**? H.G. Widdowson defines **cohesion** in his book, *Linguistics* as the ties that connect up units of language to form text and sets up a kind of connection or cohesion across the sentences. We use many techniques to join sentences together, for example, we use synonymy, place and time relaters, determiners, pronouns, pro-verbs, ellipsis, enumeration, parallelism (repetition of sentence structure) coordination and conjunctions. All these 'sentence signals' refer back or forward to neighbouring sentences. This principle is called cohesion.

We can observe cohesion not only at the level beyond sentences but also within sentences. This is achieved by the use of coordination and subordination of clauses: Coordination is especially important cohesional factor in advertising language. Look at these captions:

The Best Start for Today & Tomorrow- Bournvita

Hot wash & Hand wash, Mummy ka Double Magic –Whirlpool

Mango Fruity, Fresh and Juicy

Sandal & Cream for skin that outshines gold - LUX.

We come to understand there are different types of coordination – using coordinating conjunctions – **and, or so, but** and **parataxis.** Parataxis are short, simple clauses, often without the use of conjunctions and often sharing the same subject. In press advertising, we can observe noun group parataxis, for example, in the listing of the countries of their flight, any airline company uses:

New York – London – Paris.

Parataxis of adjective groups is also common and serves the same kind of purpose as the listing of pre-modifying adjectives in a noun group. Following example is a parataxis of separate adjectives: *New. Better. Happier.* According to Leech you find here the best example of a noun/adjective group or noun/adjective phrase.

Can you identify the best example for **parataxis** from the captions listed below?

1. *Fluent in Excellence: Emirates*
2. *I am The Bull In the Chamber: Nike*
3. *Thinking larger. Moving faster*

What we find here is the amazing technique of loading your language with maximum information. For example, in the caption ***fluent in excellence*** we find that they have eliminated all verb forms and used an adjective and a noun to make the sentence a powerful information unit. You have to understand that this sequence of words highlights more focal points of the airline than one.

Advertising language often uses the devices such as **rhyme, rhythm, alliteration and assonance** to create effect. This optimizes the effectiveness of the ad so that we remember it. It brings alive the product experience for the consumer in a compelling manner. The linguistic devices lend style and substance to the ad thus creating a lasting and meaningful experience.

Rhyme

Rhyme is a pattern of identity of sound between words or verse – lines extending from the end to the last fully accented vowel and not further. Rhyme does not refer to spelling but sounds. This is commonly used in jingles, slogans and headlines.

Pitter Patter; Pick-A-Pack; A Better Butter
Utterly Butterly Amul

Rhythm

The fundamental appeal of rhythmical language in advertising has been categorically proved. It has the advantage of powerful interlocking with consumers as it appeals to emotions as they perceive it subconsciously. Intonation, pitch and rhythm creates a synergy between the text and the consumer.

You would understand the merits when you think about 'Washing Powder Nirma'; Maggie, Noodles ... and other ads that are rhythmically loaded.

Alliteration

It is the repetition of the initial letters or sounds to produce an ornamental effect, for example, ***Sing a Song of Six Pence***. According to Greg Myers the most used consonant sounds in English are those that are made by stopping the air-stream completely (p, b, m, n, t, d, k and g) because they stand out more than others. An example of this is ***Performance, Prestige, Passion for Innovation.***

Assonance

It is the repetition of identical or similar vowel sounds, for example, foster child of silence and slow time, the L**o**ngest Line just G**o**t L**o**nger (Hercules), Soup on the Rocks (Campbell's Condensed Beef Broth) or Shop at Sear and Save.

Creating a Print Advertisement

Any advertisement whether it is print, television or online, always starts with the brief. Quite simply put, the brief is the who-why-what-where-when of the project at hand.

Who: Whom do we need to talk to? The age, geography, attitude and other characteristics of the target audience we need to address.

Why: Why are we advertising at this point? Is there a specific issue we need to address? Or is there a specific feeling we need to associate with the brand?

What: What is our brand about? What is the solution/imagery/feel that the brand/product offers in this particular context? What makes our brand different?

Where: In what media/magazine/newspaper does this advertisement appear? How can we tailor the advertisement to the specific media?

When: Is the specific period which our advertisement appears significant in any way? When do we have to finish the advertisement?

Once these answers are more or less in place, the search for the idea begins. Mostly the hint of an idea begins with any stimuli – a visual, a phrase, a song or a story. Once the ideas are shortlisted and one of them chosen, the execution kicks in. In print advertisements this involves a whole set of visual and linguistic approaches to help capture the essence of the idea in the most impressive, beautiful and memorable way. Here is where the crafting of language and the nuances of artistic execution set apart a memorable advertisement from a mediocre one.

Normally the elements of a print ad involve a headline, a visual, body copy and a tagline or a sign off. Like all rules in advertising, this list too is just indicative. Many of the best advertisements often work with one or two or even none of these elements.

Ever since the beginning, advertising has borrowed its approaches freely from art, films and other crafts. Rarely as in the case of Andy Warhol's silk screen art, it has also happened the other way. Here are some of the most common approaches in art used in everyday advertising.

Typography

Since a significant part of print advertisements involve written language, the use of good typography makes a huge difference in the communication of the idea. Today, we are seeing a revival of interest in typography with several new type foundries and type families being launched around the world.

Photography, illustration and mixed media

In the early age of advertising, illustrations were the only way to visualize an idea. Cameras were expensive and cumbersome. Thus print advertising heavily depended on illustrators to depict their products. With the arrival of professional cameras and the evolution of the photographic technique, photographs became quite synonymous with advertising. In fact, some of the most popular photographers of our century like Annie Leibovitz are inextricably associated with the advertising imagery they have created.

Currently, the proliferation of cameras has led to an over exposure of photography. Seeking a break from the photographic approach, many art directors are now seeking stylized illustrations to help them cut through the clutter of the photographs. Meanwhile many others are exploring mixed media techniques in advertising, drawing heavily from arts and traditional crafts. Either way, both photography and illustrations will remain part of print advertising.

Headlines

We need to understand that catchy headlines are very important to sell your product. Breeze through a magazine or website and list the number of ads which declares the benefits of the product through the headline. The words that you confront are amazing, introducing, suddenly and now. The language in use offers the consumer information that is very useful. Ogilvy recommends the use of the brand name in your headline.

Illustration

Creating powerful ads that get acceptance in a visible way is a qualitative task.

1. The subject of the Illustration should be supported with creative idea.
2. The use of photographs which engage the readers' curiosity is another important aspect of advertising. It should force the reader to read the copy that you have created.
3. Illustrating the end result of using the product produce the best results. Think about the Before & After campaigns in ads.
4. Using photographs to convey the powerful message is an important aspect of illustration.
5. Illustrations should be simple.
6. Advertisements using colour are much more memorable.

Body copy

The main function of body copy is to provide information about the product in an interesting manner.

1. Avoid difficult words. Use short, pithy sentences, which are easily understood. Try to make them short sentences and short paragraphs. We are not expected to write essays. But we have to give specific information about the product.
2. Use everyday language of the people. When you address the readers, they should feel that it is addressed to them personally.
3. Avoid analogies. Do not overuse superlatives.
4. You can use testimonials of celebrities.
5. Try to include the price of your product.

Layout

Readers first look at the illustration, then they examine the headline and finally the copy. So the illustration will be at the top and headline under the illustration. The copy should come under the illustration and the important point to be kept in mind is it should be simple.

As readers of print ad, let us list the way look at an ad:

1. We look at the illustration.
2. Then the headline.
3. Finally we notice the copy under the headline.
4. The caption usually includes the brand name and the promise.
5. The copy has priority over illustration
6. Three columns of type, 35 to 45 characters on an average in each column.
7. The copy may start sometime with drop-initials and very rarely used capital letters.
8. Copy is set in black and white.

Look at the news magazines and list a few print ads which have been successful in attracting readers. Analyse and critically comment on the headline, illustration, copy and their language use.

Posters

Posters transact through very powerful visuals. They deliver their messages pictorially. The brand name will be visible at a long distance.

We find unusually strong colours. But a good design should not use more than three elements in the design. Best examples available for us are Amul posters.

Typography

Typography is very essential for the people to read their copy.

1. We should never set the headlines in capital letters as readers are used to lower case.
2. One has to use full stops judiciously. Just look at the newspaper headlines. You will not find full stops in them.
3. Set the copy in a legible manner.
4. Typefaces recommended are Century family, Caslon, Baskerville and Jenson. Ogilvy recommends a few typographical devices for long copy. Use a subhead of two lines, which increases the readers' curiosity. This should come between your headline and body copy. Using the drop-initial will increase the readership. The opening paragraph should be brief. Use short lines. The important paragraphs should be in bold and italic. Use arrowheads, bullets, asterisk and marginal marks. Use numbers to highlight facts, if there are too many to relate. Recommended font size is 11.

Let us use 'The Monsoon' print advertisement for Kerala as a case study:

The brief

Six years ago, Kerala, one of India's foremost tourist destinations, was facing a tactical issue. June–July which was widely known as the off-season period was a time when travellers stayed away from the destination mostly because of the monsoon. Traditionally, the rains were not associated with holidays in India and Indians were not comfortable getting wet. The challenge at hand was to position the monsoons as a beautiful time to be in Kerala.

The print advertisement which appeared across India featured a couple in a moment of togetherness, drenched in the rain beside the famed backwaters of Kerala. The destination had never been widely shown in the rain and it brought out a new, fresh visual of the land. The models, nonchalant in the rains, inspired travellers to lose their inhibitions and come out and play in the rain. The headline, which connected the rains with intimacy and togetherness beautifully laid together the advertisement.

The results

Immediately, Kerala's monsoon season featured a rise of over 20 per cent in arrivals which has continued to increase over the years. Today, the monsoons are positioned as a valid tourist season drawing travellers from across India.

This is a print ad created by Ogilvy for *The Hindu*.
Use the case study above and comment on the various features of the print ad and the language use.

Find below two print ads created for Mazhavil Manorama. Analyse the features of the print ad; comment on the technique of minimalism.

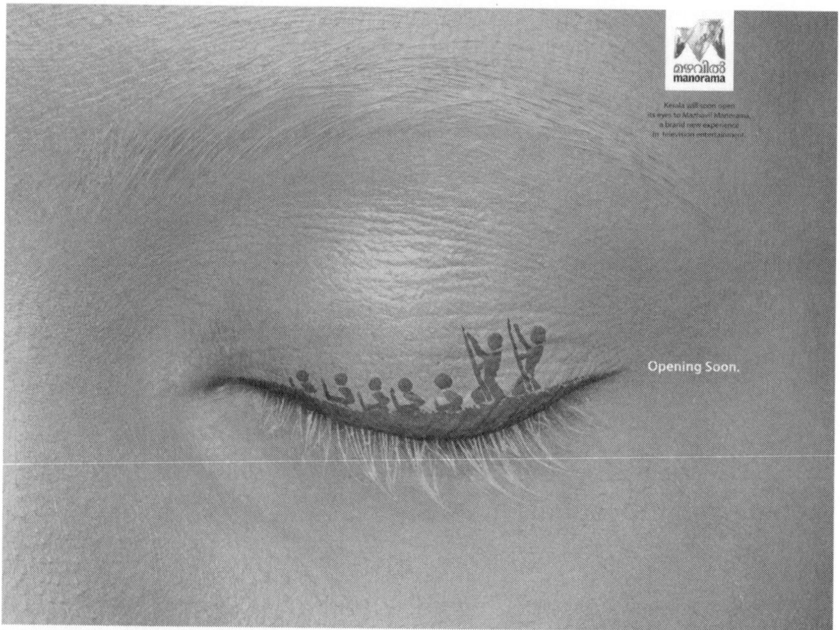

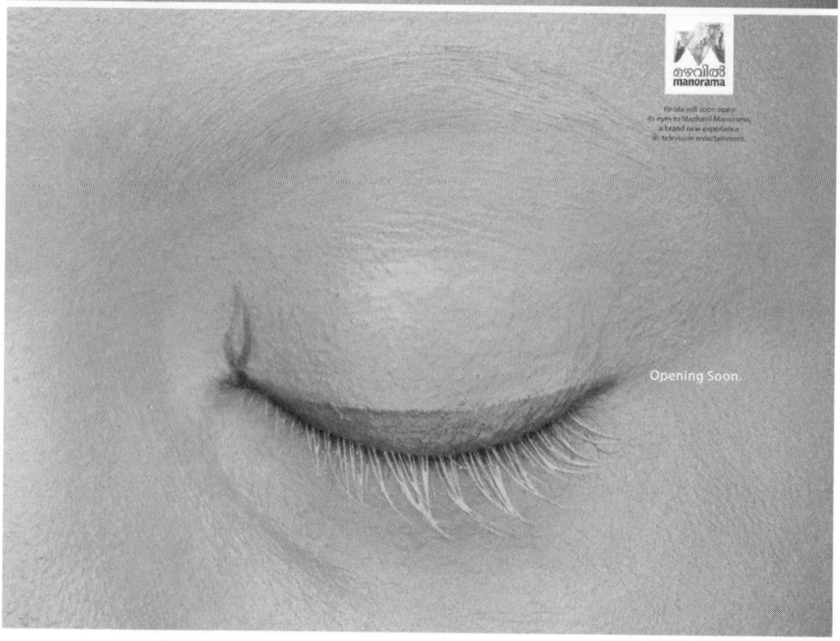

The Usage of English in Advertising in the Context of India: A Quick Overview

The Hangover

Like the early days of most other Indian commercial activities, the nature of early Indian advertising too was significantly influenced by India's colonial past. Some of the first brands that the Indian consumer encountered were imported from England. These English brands introduced an approach in advertising that revolved around the usage of 'proper' English and promoted appeals of elegance and beauty essentially European in nature. This called for advertising writers and art directors who were, in most cases, more English than the English themselves. Thus the stalwarts among advertising writers during the period were known for their formal, well-crafted – and going by today's standards – long-winded copy. Replete with idioms and imagery, these advertisements primarily catered to the affluent niche of Indian consumers to whom the 'Englishness' of the advertisement appeared to be aspirational.

The opening-up

With the widening of the market and the arrival of a whole set of Indian brands, the dynamics of English communication in the Indian market underwent a sea change. The need to communicate to a set of customers across a most diverse cultural, linguistic and geographic landscape like India called for highly creative uses of English. A large set of expensive, refined fashion, lifestyle and automobile brands continued to use formal English in their communication. Yet the need to communicate to the masses while still holding on to the elements of flair associated with English remained a massive challenge.

The Mixing-up

In the 1990s, Pepsi had used the slogan *You've got the right choice baby* featuring the legendary R&B musician Ray Charles for its promotions in the United States. Extending the same idea, it roped in Remo Fernandez, an Indian pop icon of the time to popularize the slogan in India. The reworked slogan for India which said *Yehi hai right choice baby* with its strange mix of English and Hindi was quite a success. It opened up a whole new kind of approach in the use of English in advertising. Today the 'Hinglish' approach in Indian advertising has spread to other regional markets where English is frequently seen rubbing its shoulders with many Indian regional languages – often appearing in the same advertisement or television commercial together – a curious yet effective cocktail of sorts.

The Visual Age

Another significant shift in advertising has been the one from word to visual. Extended written arguments stating the case of a brand are rarely seen these days. The visually dominant approach, once it began to be used, seemed to work particularly well in our country. Somehow, an arresting visual tied up with an interesting idea seemed to be the perfect way to get the message across to the people in a country divided (or perhaps united) by 18 official languages and hundreds of unofficial languages. Again, this led to shorter headlines and slogans that would enhance, make sense, add impact or work together with a visual. Thus the advertising writer of today is constantly challenged to make sense of the market, the target audience and keep pace with the changing usages and regional nuances while exercising his craft.

Different brands: Different approaches

Today, the use of English language in Indian or regional advertising takes several different forms. Many of the niche brands or expensive brands like high-end automobiles, perfumes and fashion accessories continue to use well-crafted formal English while brands pitched to the larger market have mostly moved into a hybrid of regional language and English.

In a study about language choice in advertising to bilinguals, the researchers asked college students in New Delhi to rate, on a seven-point scale, advertisements for detergent or chocolate, supposedly placed by multinational companies, and written in English, Hindi or a mix of the two.

'For chocolate ads, the students preferred English or an English-rich hybrid; for detergent, they preferred a Hindi-rich hybrid. The moral of the story is that well-off Indian consumers associate English with modern, cosmopolitan lifestyles, but Hindi (or presumably other local languages) has its own uses.'

In this time of change and transition, it certainly looks like the English language in Indian advertising too is all set for an interesting journey.

Glossary

Media Terms

1. **Audience:** The target group, who are the recipients/listeners/readers/viewers of a media product; their interests/likes/desires shape the content, determine vocabulary and form.
2. **Behavioural Targeting (BT):** A web media or cyber media technique which is used by websites and advertisers to target audience. A user's online behaviour (the kind of websites visited, content searched/viewed and information accessed) becomes the source of information. Based on this, the user is exposed to specific advertisements or campaigns. This is believed to be an effective method of delivering the 'right' content to the 'right' individual.
3. **B-Movie:** Film made on a low budget, featuring low paid actors or lacking star power. These are second tier movies that are cheaper to produce but which manage to bring in revenues.
4. **Cinema Verité:** Verité means truth and this term is used to refer to movies that portray reality. Such movies follow the documentary style and there is no directorial or editorial influence. Events/occurrences are shot as it unfolds.
5. **Click through:** It refers to the act of clicking or navigating to another webpage/website/advertisement/content using a link within text/editorial content or advertisement on a page.

6. **Convergence:** The coming together of technologies in new ways to create something new and better. A smart phone, for example, is a device that allows convergence of a conventional mobile phone, camera, internet, radio, chat, email, book, etc.
7. **Cowboy Shot:** A mid–thigh upwards shot, commonly used in Westerns.
8. **Demographic:** Characteristics, such as age, gender, income, education, etc., based on which the audience may be segmented.
9. **Director's Cut:** In Hollywood and in today's parlance, it popularly refers to the final version or cut of the movie that the director of the movie has complete control over. The studio or the producer has no artistic say in this version. Normally, the director is allowed six weeks time to assemble this cut. In earlier versions, DC did not contain the final music and other tracks.
10. **Establishing Shot:** The first shot in a new scene. It allows the audience to take in the place of action and helps establish location and background. It helps place the person in relation to the background or to other people in the scene.
11. **Fold:** The line that demarcates the area which can be seen when the web page loads from the area that cannot be seen on screen. Users have to scroll down to see the content below the fold.
12. **Hook:** The portion of a song that is unique and which is liked and remembered the most.
13. **Narrative:** The manner in which a programme/story/discussion is told or progresses in a way in which a story or sequence of events is put together within a text. This determines how interesting the content is. Everything from interviews and features to news analysis and films follow some form of narrative.
14. **Treatment:** A script that is longer than a synopsis but without the scope or breadth of a shooting or draft script. It includes details of every major scene, character descriptions, and in some case, a few dialogues.
15. **Vertigo Effect:** A technique from the film *Vertigo*, developed by Alfred Hitchcock. In this the camera zooms in, even while tracking backwards. This produces the effect making the person or object in focus seem stationary while the background and surroundings move/change.

16. **Voluntary Media:** Media like Twitter, Facebook and other social media sites are voluntary media. No one will be forced to visit your twitter page, what these mediums should be used for are as a means to develop an already existing relationship with your customers.
17. **Involuntary Media:** Billboards, posters, magazine ads, all come under involuntary media. The most effective of the involuntary media is print advertising. The viewer will see it as opposed to an online ad campaign where users could block your message entirely with an ad block program. Print allows you to get the reader's attention and spread your message.
18. **Continuity Script/Report:** It refers to the consistent details and logical progression from one shot to another within a scene and from one scene to another within a work. Continuity ensures that a story unfolds in a logical manner. It covers all elements like a consistent story, action, dialogue, direction, costumes, sets, props, lighting and sound. Since most films are shot out of sequence, it is particularly important that continuity be maintained. Otherwise, there will be obvious mistakes throughout the film that will distract the audience's attention away from the unfolding story. The script supervisor is responsible for ensuring that continuity is maintained throughout the shoot. After that, responsibility transfers to the editor.
19. **Green Screen:** A green chromakey screen; any chromakey process using green as the key colour. Chromakey is a process developed in the 1950s for producing travelling mattes that replaces one colour (or narrow range of colour) in an image with a new image. Chromakey is used in both film and video. In film it began as an optical effect, but is now more often produced electronically. The most common use is in televised weather reports where the reporter stands in front of a blue or green background and the background is electronically replaced with the weather information (charts, maps, live shots from out of doors, etc.). The most popular chromakey colour green, replaced the blue screen, which had been the industry standard for many years. Unlike the colour blue, green is not found in significant amounts in human skin, making it easier to separate actors from the background screen when creating visual effects.

20. **Cinematographer:** The person who is responsible for lighting and cameras on a film shoot. H/She composes each shot and directs lighting and camera operations according to the vision established by the director, advising the director on camera angles, setups, etc. Nowadays this person is called the Director of Photography (DOP) rather than the cinematographer.
21. **Censorship:** Compulsory changes made to a work by an entity other than the work's creator, usually a government body. The censor board can remove or change any part of a play, film or publication because the content is considered offensive or a threat to security. It refers to the practice of deciding that something or certain parts of something may not be broadcast, published, distributed etc., because of its content. **Pre-emptive censorship, punitive censorship** means the suppression or attempted suppression of anything regarded as objectionable.
22. **Embedded Media:** The process of combining one type of signal with another such signal in a way that both signals can be transmitted using the standard associated with just one of them. Example: Audio which is included as part of the digital video signal.
23. **Stereotypes:** A recognizable character type identified by certain key characteristics but generally lacking a fully developed personality; a one- or two-dimensional character. The comic sidekick, the tough guy with a heart of gold and the miserly old man with a heart of stone are common fictional stereotypes. Racial, ethnic and gender stereotypes are generally offensive to the group depicted.
24. **Geo Targeting:** A method of analysing what a visitor to a website is viewing or doing and deducing his or her location, then displaying custom content or advertisements accordingly.
25. **Trending:** It is a theme for bloggers that post a lot of content on a regular basis on their site. It is a pixel-perfect design for bloggers who want a new look for their site.
26. **User-generated Content:** Material posted to a website by the users of that site. It can also refer to the site itself. The content on many of these sites tends to be a mixture of original materials (both scripted and unscripted, including home movies and blogs).
27. **Avatar:** Is an incarnation of a Hindu deity. But in the world of media it means a computer generated icon or figure that represents

a character in a virtual world. It refers to an electronic image that represents and is manipulated by a computer user in a computer game.

28. **Browser:** A software program that allows a user to browse the World Wide Web.
29. **Widget:** It is an application with limited functions that can be installed and executed within a web page. A widget has the role of an auxiliary application, meaning that it just occupies a portion of a webpage and does something useful with information fetched from other websites and displayed in place. Other terms used to describe widgets are, portlet, web part, gadget, badge, module, snippet and flake. Widgets are usually created in DHTML, JavaScript or Adobe Flash.
30. **Adjacencies:** They are commercials (advertisements) which are run between two TV programmes. The commercial breaks at the beginning or end of a programme as opposed to those within the body of a programme. The individual commercials still fall within a specific programme's time slot and are sold accordingly, thus each adjacency may begin with commercial time purchased for the outgoing programme and end with commercial time purchased for the next programme on the broadcast schedule.
31. **Air shift:** Refers to the length of time in hours that a DJ works on the air at a given time. The average air shift is four hours (6 - 10 A.M., 10 AM – 2 PM, etc.) but air shifts can be up to six hours, especially for a DJ who does an early evening or overnight shift.
32. **Backsell:** Refers to the technique where the DJ announces the title and/or artist of the song he/she just played.
33. **Front sell:** This is the act of either introducing the song the DJ has begun playing. Or, it can also mean that the on-air personality has been instructed to say the name of the radio station as the very first thing h/she says on air each day.
34. **Cross fade:** The gradual transition between two audio signals; one fades out while another simultaneously fades in. It is a way of mixing from one image to another in which one image gradually fades in as another fades out. It is also known as **dissolve**.
35. **FM:** A controlled change in the frequency or pitch of a signal. A Radio frequency signal where the variations in carrier wave

frequency corresponds in proportion to the amplitude of the sounds being broadcast. The FM radio spectrum varies from 88 to 108 MHz. Television signals are actually a hybrid of FM and AM radio signals where the FM signal carries the sound information and the AM signal carries the visual information. FM signals are also used in other frequency bands for two-way communications in land mobile and marine services. FM signals are less susceptible to interference than AM broadcasts, but are limited to line-of-sight reception.

36. **AM: Amplitude Modulation** is a method of transmitting audio information using radio waves, where the frequency remains constant but the amplitude varies according to the input signal. They are analogue signals where the variations in wave amplitude (height) correspond to the information being broadcast – the wavelength, or frequency, remains the same. The original un-modulated sign wave represents the carrier signal and establishes the frequency of the AM transmission. The data signal is combined with the carrier wave to create a modulated wave that can be demodulated at the receiving end to extract the data signal from the carrier wave. The AM radio spectrum ranges from 535 to 1,705 kHz. AM radio waves broadcast from a transmitter can arrive at their destination in two forms: ground waves and sky waves.
37. **HD Radio:** A technology which transmits digital audio and data alongside existing AM and FM analogue signals. It offers FM Multicasting – the ability to broadcast multiple programme streams over a single FM frequency, It has static-free, crystal-clear reception.
38. **Middle of the Road:** Pursuing a course of action midway between extremes. Being a type of entertainment, especially popular music/film, that appeals to a wide audience.
39. **Thumbnail:** It is a small version of a picture. A thumbnail is a small image, or a part of a larger image. Normally a thumbnail will be of a border background, or a photograph. Clicking on the thumbnail image will pull up the larger original image, which can be viewed and downloaded. Use of thumbnails of background sets, borders and photographs allows more than one or two images to be shown on a web page.

40. **Special Effects:** Any unusual or artificial techniques or processes used to create the visual illusion of an altered reality (one not photographed by natural means). This includes both on-set practical or mechanical effects (miniatures, animatronics, prosthetics, atmospherics, pyrotechnics, flying effects, animation and puppets, special costumes, action props, etc.) and in camera photographic effects (split screens, process shots (rear- or front-screen projection), glass shots (using painted glass plates), slow or fast motion, etc.). Special (and visual) effects are generally used when the desired result cannot be achieved safely, conveniently or economically by other means.

References

Abercombie Nicholas. 2008. *Penguin Dictionary of Media Studies*. Penguin: New York.

Abercombie, Nicholas. 1996. *Television and Society*. Polity: Cambridge.

Belch, E George and Michael Belch. 2007. *Advertising and Promotion: An Integrated Marketing Communications Perspective by George E. Belch*. Tata McGraw Hill Publishing Company Limited: New Delhi.

Barnwell, Jane. 2008. *The Fundamentals of Film Making*. Ava Publishing: New York.

Beaman, Jim. 2006. *Programme Making for Radio*. Routledge: UK.

Berger, Arthur Asa. 1990. *Scripts: Writing for Radio and Television*. Sage Publications: New Delhi.

Bernstein, Steven. 2001. *Film Production*. Focal Press: UK.

Bignell, Jonathan. 2003. *An Introduction to Television Studies*. Routledge: London.

Branston, Gill and Roy Stafford. 2002. *The Media Student's Book*. Routledge: UK.

Chaudhuri, Arun. *Indian Advertising*. 2007. Tata McGraw Hill Publishing Company Limited: New Delhi.

Dethridge, Lisa. 2003. *Writing Your Screenplay*. Allen & Unwin: Australia.

Dictionary of Media Studies. 2006. A C Black Publishers: London.

Duncan, Tom. 2005. *Principles of Advertising & IMC*. Tata McGraw-Hill Publishing Company Ltd: New York.

Fleming, Carole. 2002. *The Radio Handbook*. Routledge: UK.

Friedmann, Anthony. 2007. *Writing for Visual Media*. Focal Press: New Delhi.

Gilmurray, Bob. 2010. *The Media Student's Guide to Radio Production*. Mightier Pen Publishing: US.

Hart, Andrew. 1991. *Understanding the Media*: A Practical Guide. Routledge: UK.

Honthaner, Eve Light. 2010. *The Complete Film Production Handbook*. Focal Press: UK.

Jones, Chris. *Guerilla Film Makers Movie Blueprint*. 2004. Continuum: New York.

Krishna Murthy, A.G. 2010. *Learnings of An Advertising Practitioner*. Tata McGraw-Hill Education Private Limited: New Delhi.

McLeish, Robert. 2005. *Radio Production*. Focal Press: UK.

McInerney, Vincent. 2001. *Writing for Radio*. Manchester University Press: New York.

Mencher, Melvin. 2008. *News Reporting and Writing*. Columbia University Press: Columbia.

Michael Newman. 2006. *Irrefutable laws of Advertising and When to Violate Them*. Wiley: New Delhi.

Murray, Michael D. 2009. *Encyclopedia of Television News*. Oryx Press: London.

Ogilvy, David. 2007. *Ogilvy on Advertising*. Carlton Publishing Group: London.

Proferes, Nicholas T. 2001. *Film directing Fundamentals: From Script to Screen*. Focal Press: UK.

Pincus, Edward and Steven Ascher. 1984. *The Filmmaker's Handbook*. Penguin Books: New York.

Reisz, Karel and Gavin Millar. 2000. *Technique of Film Editing*. Focal Press: UK.

Ries, Al and Laura Ries. 2005. *The Origin of Brands: How Product Evolution Creates Endless Possibilities for New Brands*. Collins: New York.

Rayner, Philip, Peter Wall and Stephern Kuruger. 2004. Media Studies The Essential Resource. Routledge: London.

Steele, Alexander. (ed.) 2006. *Writing Movies: The Practical Guide to Creating Stellar Screenplays*. Bloomsbury: New York.

Stradling, Linda. 2010. *Production Management for TV and Film: The Professional's Guide*. A & C Black Publishing Limited: London.

Stewart, Peter. 2006. *Essential Radio Skills: How to Present a Radio Show*. London: A & C Black Publishers Ltd .

Tiwari, Sanjay. 2003. *The (Un) Common Sense of Advertising: Getting The Basic Rights*. Response Books: New Delhi.

Trewin, Janet. 2003. *Presenting on TV and Radio: An Insider's Guide*. Focal Press: UK.

Web Resources [Accessed on 21 May 2013.]

http://abcnews.go.com/Politics/transcript-sec-state-hillary-clintons-nightline-interview-benghazi/story?id=18349660#.UZuwkqKNnxB.

http://sfy.ru/?script=kill_bill.

http://www.museum.tv/archives/etv/index.html 21 May 2013

http://minnesota.cbslocal.com/2012/12/13/full-transcript-of-frank-vascellaros-interview-with-obama/.

http://www.pastemagazine.com/blogs/lists/2012/07/the-20-best-phil-dunphy-quotes.html..

http://transcripts.cnn.com/TRANSCRIPTS/1006/01/lkl.01.html. 3.

http://www.funtrivia.com/en/subtopics/Memorable-Eastwood-Movie-Quotes-Western-Style-316097.html..

http://www.imdb.com/title/tt0055257/quotes.

http://www.socialbrite.org/sharing-center/glossary/.

http://www.radiogo.net/glossary-term-d.

http://www.imdb.com/glossary/E Web. 22 May 2013.